Revise KS3

Mathematics

Fiona Mapp

Contents

How this book will help

Attaining targets

This book is written in units linked with the attainment targets:
- **UNIT 1: Number**
- **UNIT 3: Geometry and measures**
- **UNIT 2: Algebra**
- **UNIT 4: Handling data**

Note that there is no unit linked to attainment target 1, Mathematical processes and applications. Elements of this attainment target are found throughout the book.

This Key Stage 3 Mathematics Study Guide will help you because:
- each unit starts with a checklist of the topics you need to know
- it highlights any topics that are at Level 7 and Level 8, since some of these topics may not be covered until the GCSE course
- top tips in the margin and key point panels draw your attention to important facts
- key vocabulary is written in bold
- there are plenty of examples, which you can work through
- progress checks help you to test your understanding of each topic
- the assessment questions will give you valuable practice and will help you to track your progress, since they are labelled with a National Curriculum level
- it has a glossary at the end to remind you of key words and their meaning.

Assessments and National Curriculum levels

Throughout Key Stage 3, you will have assessments in mathematics. These assessments enable both you and your teacher to see how much progress you have made. At the end of Key Stage 3, your teacher will need to decide what National Curriculum level you are working at.

During Key Stage 3, your teacher will follow a structured approach to pupil assessment in mathematics. This is referred to as APP (Assessing Pupils' Progress) and it means your teacher can:
- track your progress in mathematics
- use diagnostic information about your strengths and weaknesses
- assign you an overall National Curriculum level for mathematics at the end of Key Stage 3.

This book will help you to prepare thoroughly for these assessments.

Calculators

Most assessments usually include a non-calculator and a calculator section. Hence it is important that you have plenty of practice at non-calculator questions.

Throughout this book, this icon 🖩 highlights the questions that require a calculator. If there is no icon, they should be answered without a calculator.

Preparing for assessment

Planning

Follow these tips:
- After completing a topic in school, go through it again in this Study Guide.
- Make a note of any topics that you do not understand and go back through the notes again or ask your teacher for help.
- Use the list at the start of each unit to check the topics you have covered.

Revising

Mathematics should be revised actively – and not simply by reading:
- Revise in short bursts of about 30 minutes, followed by a short break.
- Summarise the main facts, results or formulae and highlight them.
- Try to write out key facts, and any formulae you need to learn, from memory. Check what you have written and see if there are any differences.
- Practise reading facts and formulae out loud. Learning with a friend is easier.
- Work through the examples in this guide and make sure you understand them.
- Try some examples and check your solutions (method as well as answers).
- If possible, try some questions from previous assessments and the assessment questions at the end of each chapter.
- Highlight the key words in the question, plan your answer and then go back and check that you have answered the question and that your answer is correct.

Different types of question

On mathematics papers you have several types of question:

Calculate – these questions are usually asking you to work out the answer. Remember that it is important to show full working out.

Explain – these questions are asking you to explain, with a mathematical reason or calculation, what the answer is.

Show – these questions usually require you to show, with mathematical justification, what the answer is.

Assessment technique

Remember the following points, which should help you to get through the assessment:
- Follow the instructions on the paper carefully. Make sure that you understand what any symbols mean.
- Read each question carefully, and check that you answer the question.
- Always show your working; you may pick up marks even if the answer is wrong.
- If you cannot do a question, leave it until the end. You can come back to it.
- Keep an eye on the time and complete the paper. Allow enough time to check through your answers.
- If you finish early, check everything very carefully and try to fill in any gaps.
- Try to write something even if you are not sure of it. Leaving an empty space will score you no marks. Having a go may gain you extra marks.

Number

Numbers and the number system		Studied	Revised	Assessment questions
1.1 **Numbers, powers and roots**	– Place value – Directed numbers – Factors and multiples – Prime numbers and factors – Tests of divisibility and reciprocals – Square, cube and triangular numbers – Square roots and cube roots – Indices – Index laws – Standard index form – Calculations			
1.2 **Fractions and decimals**	– Fractions – Equivalent fractions – Adding and subtracting fractions – Multiplying and dividing fractions – Fractions of quantities – Decimals – Decimals and fractions – Ordering decimals – Decimal scales – Multiplying and dividing decimals by powers of 10			
1.3 **Percentages**	– Fractions, decimals and percentages – Ordering – Percentages of a quantity – One quantity as a percentage of another – Finding a percentage increase or decrease – Profit and loss – Repeated percentage change – Reverse percentages			
1.4 **Ratio and proportion**	– Simplifying ratios – Sharing a quantity in a given ratio – Direct and inverse proportion – Best buys – Harder proportion			

Calculations		Studied	Revised	Assessment questions
2.1 **Written and calculator methods**	– Addition – Subtraction – Multiplication – Division – Order of operations – Important calculator keys – Calculating powers and reciprocals – Standard form and the calculator – Interpreting the calculator display			
2.2 **Rounding and estimating**	– Rounding numbers – Decimal places (d.p.) – Significant figures (s.f. or sig. fig.) – Possible error of half a unit when rounding – Rounding sensibly in calculations – Checking calculations – Estimating			

1 Numbers and the number system

Learning Summary

After studying this section you should be able to:

- recognise and describe number relationships including multiple, factor and square
- use and apply fractions and decimals in a variety of problems
- use and apply percentages in everyday problems
- solve problems involving ratio and proportion
- solve problems that involve calculating with powers, roots and numbers expressed in standard form

1.1 Numbers, powers and roots

Place value

Each digit in a number has a **place value**. The value of the digit depends on its place in the number.

Key Point

The place value changes by a **factor** of **10** as you **move** from one column to the next.

For example:
538 Five hundred and thirty-eight. The digit 5 represents five hundred.
2371 Two thousand, three hundred and seventy-one. The digit 7 represents seven tens or seventy.

Here are some tips for ordering whole numbers:
- Put the numbers into groups with the same number of digits.
- For each group, arrange each number in order of size depending on the place value of the digits.

Example

Arrange these numbers in order of size, smallest first:
26, 502, 794, 3297, 4209, 4351, 5, 32, 85, 114.

This becomes: 5, 26, 32, 85, 114, 502, 794, 3297, 4209, 4351

Directed numbers

Key Point

Integers are whole numbers that can be positive or negative. Positive numbers are above zero. Negative numbers are below zero. Integers are sometimes known as **directed** numbers.

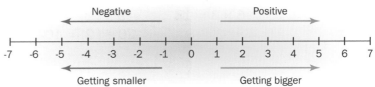

For example:

-10 is smaller than -8   so   -10 < -8
-4 is bigger than -6   so   -4 > -6
5 is bigger than -2   so   5 > -2

Directed numbers are often seen on the weather forecast in winter.
On this weather map, Aberdeen is the coldest place at -8°C and London is 6 degrees warmer than Manchester.

Adding and subtracting directed numbers

Look at the following:
The temperature at 6am was -5°C.
By 10am it had risen 8 degrees.
-5° + 8° = 3°
So the new temperature was 3°C.

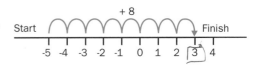

> When answering questions involving directed numbers it is useful to draw a number line to help.

Example

Find the value of -2 – 4.

-2 – 4 = -6

This represents the sign of the number.

This represents the operation of subtraction: move 4 places to the left.

Key Point

When the number to be added (or subtracted) is negative, the normal direction of movement is reversed.

When two (+) signs or two (–) signs are together, then these rules are used:

+ (+) = +
– (-) = + } Like signs give an addition

– (+) = –
+ (-) = – } Unlike signs give a subtraction

For example:
-2 + (-3) = -2 – 3 = -5   -3 – (+5) = -3 – 5 = -8
6 – (-4) = 6 + 4 = 10   5 + (-2) = 5 – 2 = 3

Multiplying and dividing directed numbers

Multiply and divide directed numbers as normal and then find the sign for the answer using the following rules.

When multiplying and dividing directed numbers:
- two like signs (both + or both –) give a positive answer
- two unlike signs (one + and the other –) give a negative answer.

For example:

$-6 \times 3 = -18$ $9 \div (-3) = -3$

$-4 \times (-2) = 8$ $-20 \div (-2) = 10$

so $^-\times + = -$

$- \times - = +$

$- \div + = -$

$- \div - = +$

$(+) \times (+) = +$
$(-) \times (-) = +$
$(+) \times (-) = -$
$(-) \times (+) = -$

$(+) \div (+) = +$
$(-) \div (-) = +$
$(+) \div (-) = -$
$(-) \div (+) = -$

Factors and multiples

If you can divide one number exactly by another number, the second number is a **factor** of the first.

For example, the factors of 12 are 1, 2, 3, 4, 6, 12.

If you multiply one number by another, the result is a **multiple** of the first number. Multiples are simply the numbers in the multiplication tables.

For example, multiples of 5 are 5, 10, 15, 20, 25, …

Prime numbers and factors

Key Point

A **prime number** has only two factors, 1 and itself.
The prime numbers up to 20 are: 2, 3, 5, 7, 11, 13, 17, 19.
Note that 1 is not a prime number.

Any positive integer can be written as a **product of prime factors**.

Example

Write 50 as a product of its prime factors. (factor tree)

The diagram can help you to find prime factors:
- Divide 50 by the first prime factor 2.
- Divide 25 by the prime factor 5.
- Keep on going until the final number is prime.

50

2   25

5   5

$50 = 2 \times 5 \times 5$
$= 2 \times 5^2$

2 is the only even prime number.

Finding the prime factors of numbers can be useful when finding the **highest common factor** (HCF) and the **lowest common multiple** (LCM) of two or more numbers.

Highest common factor (HCF)

The largest factor that two numbers have in common is called the **HCF**.

> **Example**
>
> Find the HCF of 84 and 360.
>
> First write the numbers as the products of their prime factors.
> $$84 = 2 \times 2 \quad \times 3 \quad \times 7$$
> $$360 = 2 \times 2 \times 2 \times 3 \times 3 \times 5$$
>
> Ringing the factors in common gives $2 \times 2 \times 3 = 12$
> HCF = 12.

Lowest common multiple (LCM)

The LCM of two numbers is the **lowest number** that is a **multiple** of both numbers.

> **Example**
>
> Find the LCM of 6 and 8.
>
> $$6 = \qquad 2 \times 3 = 6$$
> $$8 = 2 \times 2 \times 2 = 8$$
>
> 6 and 8 have a common prime factor of 2, which is only counted once.
> LCM of 6 and 8 is $2 \times 2 \times 2 \times 3 = 24$.

Tests of divisibility and reciprocals

To find prime numbers, simple tests of divisibility can be used, such as divisible by:

- 2 the last digit is 0, 2, 4, 6 or 8, e.g. 12, 48, 54
- 3 the sum of the digits is divisible by 3, e.g. 321 (3 + 2 + 1 = 6 and 6 is divisible by 3)
- 4 the last two digits are divisible by 4, e.g. 412 (12 is divisible by 4)
- 5 the last digit is 0 or 5, e.g. 25, 330
- 9 the sum of the digits is divisible by 9, e.g. 918 (9 + 1 + 8 = 18. 18 ÷ 9 = 2).

Key Point

The reciprocal of a number $\frac{a}{x}$ is $\frac{x}{a}$ *(flip the fractions)*

4 can be written as $\frac{4}{1}$, so the reciprocal of 4 is $\frac{1}{4}$

For example:
The reciprocal of $\frac{4}{7}$ is $\frac{7}{4}$
The reciprocal of 4 is $\frac{1}{4}$
The reciprocal of $\frac{x}{2}$ is $\frac{2}{x}$

To find the reciprocal of $1\frac{1}{2}$:
- first rewrite as an improper fraction $= \frac{3}{2}$
- reciprocal $= \frac{2}{3}$

Square, cube and triangular numbers

Square numbers

Square numbers are whole numbers raised to the power 2.

For example:
$5^2 = 5 \times 5 = 25$ (five squared)

The first 12 square numbers are:

1	4	9	16	25	36	49	64	81	100	121	144
(1 × 1)	(2 × 2)	(3 × 3)	(4 × 4)	(5 × 5)	(6 × 6)	(7 × 7)	(8 × 8)	(9 × 9)	(10 × 10)	(11 × 11)	(12 × 12)

Square numbers can be illustrated by drawing squares:

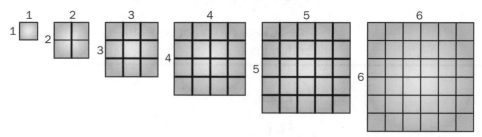

Cube numbers

Cube numbers are whole numbers raised to the power 3.

For example:
$5^3 = 5 \times 5 \times 5 = 125$ (five cubed)

Cube numbers include:

1	8	27	64	125	216	...	1000
(1 × 1 × 1)	(2 × 2 × 2)	(3 × 3 × 3)	(4 × 4 × 4)	(5 × 5 × 5)	(6 × 6 × 6)	...	(10 × 10 × 10)

Cube numbers can be illustrated by drawing cubes:

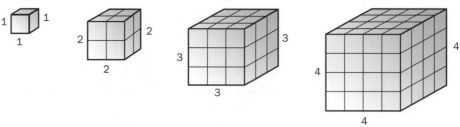

Triangular numbers

The sequence of triangular numbers is 1, 3, 6, 10, 15, ...

Each time the difference goes up by 1.

Triangular numbers can be illustrated by drawing triangle patterns:

1   3   6   10   15

6   21   →   21 is the next triangular number

Square roots and cube roots

Key Point

$\sqrt{}$ is the **square root** sign. Taking the square root is the opposite of squaring.

When a number is square-rooted it can have two square roots, **one positive** and **one negative**.

For example:
$\sqrt{25} = 5$ or -5 since $(5)^2 = 25$ and $(-5)^2 = 25$
$\sqrt{196} = \sqrt{(4 \times 49)} = 2 \times 7 = 14$

It is important to note that $\sqrt{a} + \sqrt{b}$ is not equal to $\sqrt{a + b}$.
For example, $\sqrt{9} + \sqrt{4}$ is not equal to $\sqrt{13}$. *It is equal to 6 because*
3 × 3 = 9 and 2 × 2 = 4 so 3 + 2 = 6
A **surd** is the square root of any number that is not a square number. It cannot be written exactly as a decimal.

For example:
$\sqrt{2}, \sqrt{3}, \sqrt{5}, \sqrt{6}, \sqrt{7}, \ldots$ are all surds.

> **Example**
>
> Write $\sqrt{18}$ in terms of the simplest possible surd.
>
> $\sqrt{18} = \sqrt{9} \times \sqrt{2}$
> $\quad\quad = 3 \times \sqrt{2} = 3\sqrt{2}$

Look for the highest possible square factor.

Key Point

$\sqrt[3]{}$ is the **cube root** sign. Taking the cube root is the opposite of cubing.

For example:
$\sqrt[3]{27} = 3$ since $3 \times 3 \times 3 = 27$

$\sqrt[3]{-125} = -5$ since $-5 \times -5 \times -5 = -125$

The cube root of a positive number is positive.
The cube root of a negative number is negative.

Indices

Key Point

An **index** (plural: indices) is sometimes called a **power**. It can be written as:

The base $\longrightarrow a^b \longleftarrow$ The index or power

The base is the value that has to be multiplied. The index indicates how many times.

For example:
6^4 is read as '6 to the power of 4'. It means $6 \times 6 \times 6 \times 6$.
2^7 is read as '2 to the power of 7'. It means $2 \times 2 \times 2 \times 2 \times 2 \times 2 \times 2$.

remember! 6

20/12/11

12/5

Index laws

There are several laws of indices:

1 When multiplying, **add** the powers. *eg* $4^2 \times 4^6$

$4^3 \times 4^2 = (4 \times 4 \times 4) \times (4 \times 4)$

$= 4 \times 4 \times 4 \times 4 \times 4$ $= 4^{(2+6)}$

$= 4^5$ i.e. $4^{(3+2)}$

2 When dividing, **subtract** the powers.

$6^5 \div 6^2 = (6 \times 6 \times 6 \times 6 \times 6) \div (6 \times 6)$

$= 6 \times 6 \times 6$

$= 6^3$ i.e. $6^{(5-2)}$

3 Any number raised to the power zero is just 1, provided the number is not zero.

$7^5 \div 7^5 = 7^{5-5} = 7^0 = 1$

$5^0 = 1 \qquad 2.7189^0 = 1$

0^0 is undefined (has no meaning).

4 Any number raised to the power 1 is just itself.

$15^1 = 15 \qquad 1923^1 = 1923$ *eg* $256^1 = 256.$ *because you're*

×'s it by you

The above rules also apply when the powers are negative.

For example: $\times = \frac{(2)}{(1)}$ *big - small*

$6^{-2} \times 6^{12} = 6^{10}$

$8^{-4} \div 8^3 = 8^{-7}$ $\div = \frac{(1)}{(2)}$ $(+)$

$7^0 = 1$

5 (Level 8) Any number raised to a negative power just turns it upside down and makes the power positive.

> When the index is negative, always remember to take the reciprocal first.

For example:

$2^{-4} = \dfrac{1}{2^4} = \dfrac{1}{16}$

$3^{-2} = \dfrac{1}{3^2} = \dfrac{1}{9}$

6 (Level 8) A fractional power is a root.

For example:

$4^{\frac{1}{2}} = \sqrt{4} = 2$

$27^{\frac{1}{3}} = \sqrt[3]{27} = 3$

Standard index form

(Level 8) **Standard index form** (standard form) is a special form of index notation and is used to write very large or very small numbers in a simpler way.

Key Point

When written in standard form, the number will be written as:

$$a \times 10^n$$

a must lie between 1 and 10, that is $1 \leqslant a < 10$. n is the power of 10 by which you multiply (if n is positive), or divide (if n is negative). If the number is large, n is positive; if the number is small, n is negative.

Large numbers

If the number is large, n is positive.

For example:
$$6\,3\,4\,0\,0\,0 = 6.34 \times 10^5$$
$$2730 = 2.73 \times 10^3$$

Small numbers

If the number is small, n is negative.

For example:
$$0.0\,0\,0\,4\,6 = 4.6 \times 10^{-4}$$
$$0.0361 = 3.61 \times 10^{-2}$$

Calculations

The calculator can be used to do complex calculations when the numbers are in standard form.

Key Point

The $\boxed{\text{EXP}}$, $\boxed{\text{EE}}$ or $\boxed{\times 10^x}$ key puts the ×10 part into the calculation.

For example:
$$(2.6 \times 10^3) \times (8.9 \times 10^{12}) = 2.314 \times 10^{16}$$

This is keyed in as $\boxed{2.6}\ \boxed{\text{EXP}}\ \boxed{3}\ \boxed{\times}\ \boxed{8.9}\ \boxed{\text{EXP}}\ \boxed{12}\ \boxed{=}$

and the display will usually show 2.314×10^{16} or 2.314^{16}

When working without a calculator, the laws of indices can be used to multiply and divide numbers written in standard form.

If carrying out a calculation involving standard form on a calculator, remember to put the ×10 part into your answer. A display of 2.314^{16} must be written as 2.314×10^{16}

Examples

(a) Work out $(2.4 \times 10^{-4}) \times (3 \times 10^7)$
$$= (2.4 \times 3) \times (10^{-4} \times 10^7)$$
$$= 7.2 \times 10^{-4 + 7}$$
$$= 7.2 \times 10^3$$

(b) Work out $(12.4 \times 10^{-4}) \div (4 \times 10^7)$
$$= (12.4 \div 4) \times (10^{-4} \div 10^7)$$
$$= 3.1 \times 10^{-4 - 7}$$
$$= 3.1 \times 10^{-11}$$

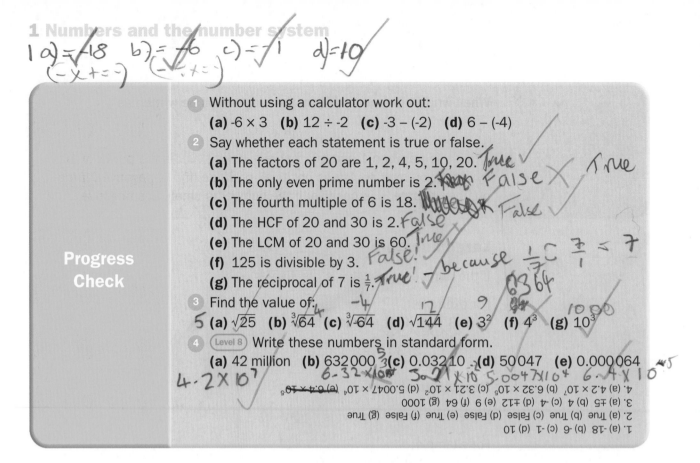

(handwritten top) 1 a) = -18 b) = -6 c) = 1 d) = 10 (- × + = -) (- ÷ + = -)

Progress Check

1 Without using a calculator work out:
   (a) -6 × 3   **(b)** 12 ÷ -2   **(c)** -3 − (-2)   **(d)** 6 − (-4)

2 Say whether each statement is true or false.
   (a) The factors of 20 are 1, 2, 4, 5, 10, 20. *True*
   (b) The only even prime number is 2. *False*   *True*
   (c) The fourth multiple of 6 is 18. *False*
   (d) The HCF of 20 and 30 is 2. *False*
   (e) The LCM of 20 and 30 is 60. *True*
   (f) 125 is divisible by 3. *False!*
   (g) The reciprocal of 7 is $\frac{1}{7}$. *True! — because $\frac{1}{7}$ ⊂ $\frac{7}{1}$ = 7*

3 Find the value of: *−4   12   9   64   1000*
   (a) $\sqrt{25}$ **(b)** $\sqrt[3]{64}$ **(c)** $\sqrt[3]{-64}$ **(d)** $\sqrt{144}$ **(e)** 3^2 **(f)** 4^3 **(g)** 10^3

4 (Level 8) Write these numbers in standard form.
   (a) 42 million   **(b)** 632 000   **(c)** 0.032 10   **(d)** 50 047   **(e)** 0.000 064
   4.2 × 10⁷   6.32 × 10⁵   3.21 × 10   5.0047 × 10⁴   6.4 × 10⁵

Answers (printed upside down):
4. (a) 4.2 × 10⁷ (b) 6.32 × 10⁵ (c) 3.21 × 10² (d) 5.0047 × 10⁴ (e) 6.4 × 10⁵
3. (a) ±5 (b) 4 (c) -4 (d) ±12 (e) 9 (f) 64 (g) 1000
2. (a) True (b) True (c) False (d) False (e) True (f) False (g) True
1. (a) -18 (b) -6 (c) -1 (d) 10

1.2 Fractions and decimals

Fractions

A fraction is part of a whole number. $\frac{2}{5}$ means 2 parts out of 5.

The top number is called the **numerator**; the bottom number is the **denominator**.

A fraction like $\frac{2}{5}$ is called a **proper fraction** because the denominator is greater than the numerator. A fraction like $\frac{15}{7}$ is called an **improper fraction** because the numerator is greater than the denominator.

A fraction like $1\frac{5}{7}$ is called a **mixed number**.

Equivalent fractions

Equivalent fractions are fractions that have the same value. Fractions can be changed into their **equivalent** by either multiplying or dividing the numerator and denominator by the same number.

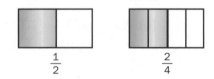

$$\frac{1}{2} \qquad \frac{2}{4}$$

From the diagram it can be seen that $\frac{1}{2} = \frac{2}{4}$.

(handwritten top-left)
$$\frac{5^{x}}{7} + \frac{1}{14} = \frac{11}{14}$$ 10

(handwritten top-right) 17 6 102 4

Examples

(a) $\frac{5}{7} = \frac{?}{35}$

$$\overset{\times 5}{\frac{5}{7} = \frac{25}{35}}\underset{\times 5}{}$$

> Multiply the numerator and denominator by 5.

(b) $\frac{40}{50} = \frac{?}{5}$

$$\overset{\div 10}{\frac{40}{50} = \frac{4}{5}}\underset{\div 10}{}$$

> Divide the numerator and denominator by 10.

Key Point

Fractions can be **simplified** if the numerator and the denominator have a common factor.

Examples

(a) Write as simply as possible: $\frac{12}{18}$

$$\overset{\div 6}{\frac{12}{18} = \frac{2}{3}}\underset{\div 6}{}$$

Since 6 is the highest common factor of 12 and 18, divide both the numerator and the denominator by 6. This process is known as **cancelling**.

(b) Place in order $\frac{7}{8}, \frac{4}{5}$ and $\frac{11}{20}$, smallest first.

The common denominator of 8, 5 and 20 is 40 (40 is the **LCM** of 8, 5 and 20).

$$\frac{7}{8} = \frac{35}{40} \qquad \frac{4}{5} = \frac{32}{40} \qquad \frac{11}{20} = \frac{22}{40}$$

In order, smallest first: $\frac{22}{40}, \frac{32}{40}, \frac{35}{40}$

$$\Rightarrow \frac{11}{20}, \frac{4}{5}, \frac{7}{8}$$

> By converting fractions to a **common denominator**, they can be easily placed in order.

(handwritten, left margin)
$$\frac{5}{7} + \frac{1}{14} = \frac{}{14}$$
① LCD of 14 and 7 = 14
so $\overline{14}$.
② $\frac{}{14} \div 7 = 2$ so $\frac{5}{7}$
then 2×5 from $\frac{5}{7}$ = 10
③ $\frac{}{14} \div \overline{14} = 1$ so
the answer is
$\frac{11}{14}$ (because 10 + 1 = 11)

Adding and subtracting fractions

Only fractions with the same denominator can be added or subtracted.

(handwritten, left margin)
$$\frac{1}{8} + \frac{3}{4} = \frac{1+6}{8} = \frac{7}{8}$$ (×2)
$$\frac{3}{16} = \frac{10+3}{16} = \frac{7}{16}$$

Examples

(a) Work out $\frac{1}{8} + \frac{3}{4}$

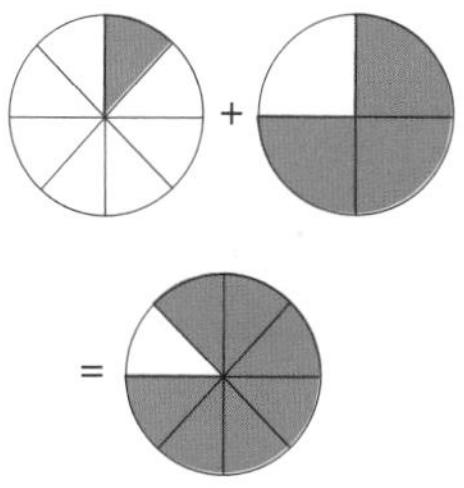

The lowest common denominator of 8 and 4 is 8. Replacing $\frac{3}{4}$ with $\frac{6}{8}$ gives:

$$\frac{1}{8} + \frac{6}{8} = \frac{7}{8}$$

> Only add the numerators; the denominator stays the same.

$$\overset{\times 2}{\frac{3}{4} = \frac{6}{8}}\underset{\times 2}{}$$

(b) Work out $\frac{5}{8} - \frac{3}{16}$

$$\frac{10}{16} - \frac{3}{16} = \frac{7}{16}$$

> 16 is the lowest common denominator of 8 and 16.

$$\overset{\times 2}{\frac{5}{8} = \frac{10}{16}}\underset{\times 2}{}$$

Multiplying and dividing fractions

To multiply fractions, multiply the numerators together and multiply the denominators together. Try cancelling before multiplying. Any mixed or whole numbers need to be written as improper fractions before starting.

For example:

- $\frac{2}{5} \times \frac{1}{9} = \frac{2}{45}$

- $\frac{4}{7} \times \frac{2}{11} = \frac{8}{77}$

- $\frac{5}{7} \times 1\frac{1}{2} = \frac{5}{7} \times \frac{3}{2} = \frac{15}{14} = 1\frac{1}{14}$

To divide fractions, change the division into a multiplication by taking the **reciprocal** of the second fraction (turning it upside down) and multiplying both fractions together.

> Cancelling can make the calculation easier.

Example

Work out $\frac{7}{9} \div \frac{5}{18}$

$= \frac{7}{9_1} \times \frac{18^2}{5}$ ← Take the reciprocal of $\frac{5}{18}$ and multiply it with the $\frac{7}{9}$.

$= \frac{14}{5} = 2\frac{4}{5}$ ← Write the final answer as a mixed number.

Fractions of quantities

Key Point — To find a fraction of a quantity, you **multiply** the fraction with the quantity.

> You can find $\frac{1}{8}$ by dividing by 8 and then $\frac{3}{8}$ by multiplying by 3.

Example

In a survey of 24 pupils, $\frac{3}{8}$ prefer English, $\frac{1}{6}$ prefer Art and the rest prefer Maths. How many students prefer Maths?

English $\quad \frac{3}{8} \times 24 = 9 \quad$ 24 ÷ 8 × 3

Art $\quad\quad \frac{1}{6} \times 24 = 4$

$\quad\quad\quad\quad$ Total = 13

Hence 24 − 13 = 11 pupils prefer Maths.

Decimals

A decimal point is used to separate whole number columns from fraction columns.

For example:

Thousands	Hundreds	Tens	Units		Tenths	Hundredths	Thousandths
6	7	1	4	·	2	3	8

Decimal point

Decimals and fractions

Key Point

To change a fraction into a decimal, **divide** the numerator by the denominator, either by short division or by using a calculator.

To change a decimal into a fraction, write the decimal as a fraction with a denominator of 10, 100, etc. (look at the last decimal place to decide) and then cancel.

For example:

- $\frac{2}{5} = 2 \div 5 = 0.4$
- $0.23 = \frac{23}{100}$

  Last d.p. is 'hundredths' so the denominator is 100.

- $\frac{1}{8} = 1 \div 8 = 0.125$
- $0.165 = \frac{165}{1000} = \frac{33}{200}$

  Last d.p. is 'thousandths' so the denominator is 1000.

Decimals that never stop and have a repeating pattern are called **recurring** decimals. All fractions give either **terminating** or **recurring** decimals.

For example:

A dot is placed over the first and last numbers that repeat.

$\frac{1}{3} = 0.333\,333\ldots$ usually written as $0.\dot{3}$

$\frac{5}{11} = 0.454\,5454\ldots$ $= 0.\dot{4}\dot{5}$

$\frac{4}{7} = 0.\dot{5}71\,428\,571\ldots$ $= 0.\dot{5}71\,42\dot{8}$

(Level 8) Recurring decimals can be changed into fractions.

Example

Change $0.\dot{2}$ into a fraction in its lowest terms.

Let $x = 0.222\,222\ldots$ ①
then $10x = 2.222\,222\ldots$ ②

Practise these by checking on a calculator.

Multiply by 10^n, where n is the length of the recurring pattern. In this example, $n = 1$.

Subtract equation ① from equation ②. This has the effect of making the recurring pattern disappear:

     $9x = 2$
       $x = \frac{2}{9}$ Divide both sides by 9.

Ordering decimals

Key Point

When ordering decimals:
- first write them with the same number of figures after the decimal point
- then compare whole numbers, **digits** in the tenths place, digits in the hundredths place, and so on.

Example

Arrange these numbers in order of size, smallest first:
5.29, 5.041, 5.7, 2.93, 5.71

2.93, 5.04 5.29, 5.7, 5.71

First rewrite them to the same number of d.p.:
5.290, 5.041, 5.700, 2.930, 5.710

Then reorder them:
2.930, 5.041, 5.290, 5.700, 5.710

> The zero is smaller than the 1.

Rewrite in original form:
2.93, 5.041, 5.29, 5.7, 5.71

Decimal scales

Decimals are usually used when reading scales. Measuring jugs, rulers and weighing scales are examples of scales that have decimals.

For example:

There are 10 spaces between the 8 and the 9. Each space is 0.1

There are five spaces between the 6 and the 7. Each space is 0.2

There are four spaces between the 12 and the 13. Each space is 0.25

Multiplying and dividing decimals by powers of 10

To multiply decimals by 10, 100, 1000, ... etc. move each digit one, two or three places to the left.

For example:

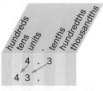

4 units × 10 = 40
3 tenths × 10 = 3 units

16 420 ← × 10 000
16.42 ← × 10
1.642
164.2 ← × 100
1642 ← × 1000

To divide decimals by 10, 100, 1000, ... etc. move each digit one, two or three places to the right.

For example:

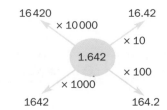

0.017 35 ← ÷ 10 000
1.735 ← ÷ 100
173.5
17.35 ← ÷ 10
0.1735 ← ÷ 1000

Key Point

When **multiplying** by a number between **0 and 1**, the answer is **smaller** than the starting value.

For example:

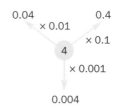

```
        0.04              0.4
            × 0.01      
                        × 0.1
              4
                  × 0.001
```

0.004

Key Point

When **dividing** by a number between **0 and 1**, the answer is **bigger** than the starting value.

For example:

```
        400               40
            ÷ 0.01
                        ÷ 0.1
              4
                  ÷ 0.001
```

4000

Progress Check

1. Place these fractions in order, smallest first.
   $\frac{1}{2}, \frac{2}{7}, \frac{5}{14}, \frac{3}{28}$ *3/28 2/7 5/14 1/2*

2. Change these fractions into decimals. 🖩
   (a) $\frac{5}{9}$ **(b)** $\frac{4}{5}$ **(c)** $\frac{6}{13}$ *0.5   0.8   0.4454*

3. Which is the correct answer to $\frac{2}{9} \div \frac{1}{3}$?
   A $\frac{2}{27}$ **B** $\frac{2}{3}$ **C** $\frac{3}{12}$ **D** $\frac{6}{27}$ *B*

4. In a class of 32 pupils, $\frac{3}{4}$ are right-handed. How many pupils are left-handed?   *8*

5. Arrange these decimals in order of size, smallest first:
   0.046, 0.032, 0.471, 0.4702, 0.4694   *0.032, 0.046, 0.4694, 0.4702, 0.471*

6. (Level 8) Change $0.\dot{7}$ into a fraction.

7. Fill in the spaces below:

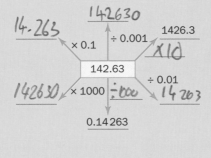

```
                    142630
    14.263          ÷ 0.001      1426.3
         × 0.1               ×10
                142.63
                        ÷ 0.01
   142630  × 1000  ÷ 000   14263
                0.14263
```

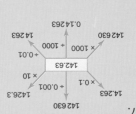

7.
```
                           0.14263
              14263                    142630
                      × 1000  ÷ 1000
                           ÷ 0.01
                           142.63
                   × 10
              1426.3  ÷ 0.001   × 0.1   14.263
                           142630
```

1. $\frac{3}{28}, \frac{2}{7}, \frac{5}{14}, \frac{1}{2}$ 2. (a) 0.5̇ (b) 0.8 (c) 0.461538 3. **B** $\frac{2}{3}$
4. 8 pupils 5. 0.032, 0.046, 0.4694, 0.4702, 0.471 6. $\frac{7}{9}$

21

2/1/2012

1.3 Percentages

A **percentage** is a fraction with a **denominator of 100**.
% is the percentage sign.

For example: simplifying
75% means $\frac{75}{100}$ (equivalent to $\frac{3}{4}$).

25%

75%

Example

A flag has three colours: red, white and blue.
If 30% is red and 45% is blue, what percentage is white?

30 + 45 = 75%

Rest is white   100 − 75 = 25%

Fractions, decimals and percentages

Fractions, decimals and percentages are different ways of expressing parts of a whole quantity.

To change a **percentage** into a **decimal**, first write as a fraction with a denominator of 100 and then divide the numerator by the denominator.

For example: eg $23\% = \frac{23}{100} = 0.23$
$12\% = \frac{12}{100} = 0.12$ percentage fraction decimal

To change a **fraction** or **decimal** into a percentage, multiply by 100%.

For example:
$\frac{2}{5} = \frac{2}{5} \times 100\% = \frac{200}{5}\% = 40\%$

numerator
divided by the
denominator.

→ ×100

Fraction	Decimal	Percentage
$\frac{1}{2}$	0.5	50%
$\frac{1}{3}$	$0.\dot{3}$	$33.\dot{3}\%$
$\frac{2}{3}$	$0.\dot{6}$	$66.\dot{6}\%$
$\frac{1}{4}$	0.25	25%
$\frac{3}{4}$	0.75	75%
$\frac{1}{5}$	0.2	20%
$\frac{1}{8}$	0.125	12.5%
$\frac{3}{8}$	0.375	37.5%
$\frac{1}{10}$	0.1	10%
$\frac{1}{100}$	0.01	1%

1 ÷ 4 →   × 100% →

You need to learn these common fractions and their equivalents.

Ordering

When putting fractions, decimals and percentages in order of size, it is best to change them all to **decimals** first.

Example

Place in order of size, smallest first:

$\frac{1}{4}$, 0.241, 29%, 64%, $\frac{1}{3}$

0.25, 0.241, 0.29, 0.64, 0.$\dot{3}$ — Put into decimals first.

0.241, 0.25, 0.29, 0.$\dot{3}$, 0.64 — Now order.

0.241, $\frac{1}{4}$, 29%, $\frac{1}{3}$, 64% — Now rewrite in the original form.

Percentages of a quantity

Key Point

The word **'of'** means **multiply**. When calculating a percentage of a quantity using a mental method, find 10% or 1% first.

VAT (value added tax) is charged at 17.5% and can be calculated mentally using the same method.

Example

(a) Find 15% of £650 without using a calculator.

$10\% = \frac{1}{10}$ so $\frac{650}{10} = £65$
5% is half of 65 = £32.50
15% = 65 + 32.50
   = £97.50

$650 \div 10 = 65 = 10\%$

$65 \div 2$ because

$\frac{1}{2}$ of 10% is 5% and

$10 + 5 = 15\%$

$65 \div 2 = 52.50$

so $65 + 32.50$

$= 97.50$ -

97.50

(b) Find 17.5% of £320.

to get to
again

10% = 320 ÷ 10 = £32
5% = £16
2.5% = £8
So 17.5% = 32 + 16 + 8 = £56

Key Point

When finding a percentage of a quantity with a calculator, multiply by the percentage and divide by 100.

Example

Find 12% of £20.

$\frac{12}{100} \times £20 = £2.40$

[20] [×] [12] [÷] [100] [=]

One quantity as a percentage of another

To find one quantity as a percentage of another, divide the first quantity by the second quantity and multiply by 100%.

> Make a fraction with the two numbers. Multiply by 100% to get a percentage.

Example *calculator*

A survey showed that 42 people out of 65 preferred salt and vinegar flavoured crisps. What percentage preferred salt and vinegar crisps?

$\frac{42}{65} \times 100\% = 64.6\%$ (1 d.p.)

Finding a percentage increase or decrease

Percentages often appear in real-life problems. If a quantity is increased by a percentage, then that percentage of the quantity is added to the original. If a quantity decreases by a percentage, then that percentage of the quantity is subtracted from the original.

Example

Two years ago the average price of a 3-bedroom house was £159 000. Since then the average price of a 3-bedroom house has risen by 35%. Work out the average price now.

100% = £159 000
Increase = 35% of £159 000
$= \frac{35}{100} \times £159\,000$
$= £55\,650$

Average price is now
£159 000 + £55 650
$= £214\,650$

This is the same as multiplying £159 000 by $1 + \frac{35}{100}$ or 1.35:
£159 000 × 1.35
$= £214\,650$

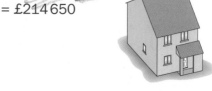

Key Point

To find the result of a percentage increase, multiply by (1 + the percentage divided by 100).

Example

A new car was bought for £8600. After two years it had lost 30% of its value. Work out the value of the car after two years.

100% = £8600
10%   = 8600 ÷ 10 = £860
30%   = 860 × 3 = £2580

This is the same as multiplying 8600 by $1 - \frac{30}{100}$ or 0.7:
8600 × 0.7 = £6020

Value of car after two years:
original − decrease
£8600 − £2580 *because*
$= £6020$ *decrease*

> **Key Point**
>
> To find the result of a percentage decrease, multiply by (1 – the percentage divided by 100).

Profit and loss

(Level 7) If you buy an article, the price you pay is the **cost price**. If you sell the article, the price you sell it for is the **selling price**. **Profit (or loss)** is the difference between the cost price and the selling price.

> **Key Point**
>
> The profit or loss can be written as a percentage of the original price:
>
> $$\text{Percentage profit} = \frac{\text{profit}}{\text{original price}} \times 100\%$$
>
> $$\text{Percentage loss} = \frac{\text{loss}}{\text{original price}} \times 100\%$$

Examples

(a) A shop bought a cooker for £350. A customer later buys the cooker for £530. Find the percentage profit.

Profit = £530 – £350
  = £180

> Remember to divide by the original value.

$$\text{Percentage profit} = \frac{\text{profit}}{\text{original price}} \times 100\%$$

180 ÷ 350

$$= \frac{180}{350} \times 100\% = 51\% \text{ profit (nearest \%)}$$

(b) Jackie bought a bed for £730. She later sold it for £420. Calculate her percentage loss.

Loss = £730 – £420
  = £310   *310*

$$\text{Percentage loss} = \frac{310}{730} \times 100\% = 42.5\% \text{ loss (1 d.p.)}$$

Repeated percentage change

(Level 7) Questions on repeated percentage change involve the change in value over a period of time.

Examples

decreased price

(a) A car was bought for £8000. Each year it depreciated in value by 20%. What was the car worth three years later?

> Do not do 3 × 20% = 60% reduction over three years.

Method 1

Find 80% of the value of the car first.

Year 1: $\frac{80}{100} \times £8000 = £6400$

Then work out the value year by year.

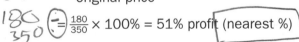

£6400 depreciates in value by 20%

Year 2: $\frac{80}{100} \times £6400 = £5120$

Year 3: $\frac{80}{100} \times £5120 = £4096$ after three years ◄ £5120 depreciates by 20%

Method 2

A quick way to work this out is to use the multiplier method. Finding 80% of the value of the car is the same as multiplying by 0.8. 0.8 is the **multiplier**.

Year 1: $0.8 \times 8000 = £6400$
Year 2: $0.8 \times 6400 = £5120$
Year 3: $0.8 \times 5120 = £4096$

This is the same as working out $(0.8)^3 \times 8000 = £4096$, which is much quicker.

(b) Jonathan has £2500 in his savings account and compound interest is paid at 4.4% per annum (per year). How much will he have in his account after three years?

Year 1:
$1 + \frac{4.4}{100}$ is the multiplier
$1.044 \times 2500 = £2610$

Year 2:
$1.044 \times 2610 = £2724.84$

Year 3:
$1.044 \times 2724.84 = £2844.73$ (to the nearest penny)
Total = £2844.73 (to the nearest penny)
This could have been calculated as $(1.044)^3 \times 2500$.

> **Compound interest** is an example of repeated percentage change because interest is paid on the interest earned as well as on the original amount.

Reverse percentages

(Level 8) Reverse percentage is when the **original** quantity is calculated.

Example

The price of a television is reduced by 20% in the sales. It now costs £840. What was the original price?

The sale price is 100% − 20% = 80% of the original price.
$\frac{80}{100} = 0.8$
$0.8 \times$ original price = £840
$\qquad$ original price $= \frac{840}{0.8} = £1050$

$$\text{original price} \xrightarrow{\times 0.8} \text{new price}$$
$$\text{original price} \xleftarrow{\div 0.8} \text{new price}$$

> Check the answer is sensible and that it is more than the sale price.

Key Point

To find the value before a percentage increase, divide by (1 + the percentage divided by 100).
To find the value before a percentage decrease, divide by (1 − the percentage divided by 100).

Progress Check ✗

1. Change to fractions and decimals: 🔲
   (a) 20% **(b)** 32% **(c)** 85% **(d)** 210%
2. A meal costs £84. VAT at 17.5% is added to the cost of the meal. How much does the meal cost including VAT?
3. Thomas got 62 out of 80 in a test. What percentage is this? 🔲
4. (Level 7) A house was bought for £165 000. Three years later it was sold for £190 000. Work out the percentage profit. 🔲
5. (Level 8) 15 000 people visited a museum this year. This was an increase of 20% on last year. How many visitors were there last year? 🔲

1. (a) $\frac{1}{5}$, 0.2 (b) $\frac{8}{25}$, 0.32 (c) $\frac{17}{20}$, 0.85 (d) $2\frac{1}{10}$, 2.1   2. £98.70   3. 77.5%   4. 15.2% (1 d.p.)   5. 12 500

1.4 Ratio and proportion

Simplifying ratios

A **ratio** is used to compare two or more related quantities. '**Compared to**' is replaced with two dots :

For example, '16 boys compared to 20 girls' can be written as 16 : 20. To simplify ratios, divide both parts of the ratio by the highest common factor. Here is an example:

16 : 20 = 4 : 5 ← Divide both parts by 4.

> Ratio and proportion appear in many areas of mathematics so try to understand the methods shown.

Examples

(a) Simplify the ratio 21 : 28

= 3 : 4 ← Divide both parts by 7.

(b) Express the ratio 5 : 2 in the ratio n : 1

5 : 2 = $\frac{5}{2}$: $\frac{2}{2}$ ← Divide both parts by 2.

= 2.5 : 1

Sharing a quantity in a given ratio

Key Point

To divide in a ratio:
- add up the total parts
- work out what one part is worth
- work out what the other parts are worth.

Example

A business makes a profit of £32 000. The profit is divided between the directors in the ratio 3 : 2 : 5. How much do they each receive?

3 + 2 + 5 = 10 parts
10 parts = £32 000
1 part = $\frac{£32\,000}{10}$
1 part = £3200

So the directors get: 3 × 3200 = £9600
2 × 3200 = £6400
5 × 3200 = £16 000

Check: the total should equal £32 000.

Direct and inverse proportion

Two quantities are in **direct proportion** if their ratios stay the same when the quantities increase or decrease.

Examples

(a) A picture of length 12cm is to be enlarged in the ratio 7 : 3. What is the length of the enlarged picture?

Divide 12cm by 3 to get 1 part:
12 ÷ 3 = 4cm
Multiply this by 7 to get the length of the enlarged picture: 4 × 7 = 28cm

12cm

(b) A recipe for 4 people needs 1600g of flour. How much is needed for 6 people?

FLOUR

Divide 1600g by 4, so 400g for 1 person.
Multiply by 6, so 6 × 400g = 2400g for 6 people.

Two quantities are in **inverse proportion** if one increases at the same rate as the other decreases.

Example

It took 8 people 6 days to build a wall. At the same rate, how long would it take 3 people?

Time for 8 people = 6 days
Time for 1 person = 6 × 8 = 48 days
Time for 3 people = $\frac{48}{3}$
= 16 days

It takes 1 person longer to build the wall.

3 people will take $\frac{1}{3}$ the time taken by 1 person.

Best buys

Unit amounts can be used to work out 'best buys', i.e. which is the better value for money.

Example

The same brand of coffee is sold in two different-sized jars. Which jar represents the better value for money?

POTS Coffee 100g £1.86

POTS Coffee 250g £3.47

Find the cost per gram for both jars:
100g costs 186p so 186 ÷ 100 = 1.86p per gram.
250g costs 347p so 347 ÷ 250 = 1.388p per gram.

Since the larger jar costs less per gram, it is the better value for money.

Harder proportion

(Level 8) The notation $\propto$ means '**is directly proportional to**'. This is often abbreviated to 'is proportional to'.

$y \propto x$ means that when x is multiplied by a number, then so is the corresponding value of y. For example:

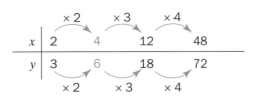

$$\begin{array}{c|cccc} & \times 2 & \times 3 & \times 4 \\ x & 2 & 4 & 12 & 48 \\ \hline y & 3 & 6 & 18 & 72 \\ & \times 2 & \times 3 & \times 4 \end{array}$$

If $y \propto x^2$, when x is multiplied by a number, y is multiplied by the square of the number.

$y \propto \frac{1}{x}$ means that y is **inversely proportional** to x. When x is multiplied by a number, then y is divided by that number, and vice versa. For example:

$$\begin{array}{c|cccc} & \times 4 & \times 3 & \div 2 \\ x & 4 & 16 & 48 & 24 \\ \hline y & 12 & 3 & 1 & 2 \\ & \div 4 & \div 3 & \times 2 \end{array}$$

Progress Check

1. Three bars of chocolate cost £1.20. How much will four bars cost? £1.60
2. A boy spent his savings of £40 on books and DVDs in the ratio 1 : 3. How much did he spend on DVDs? £30
3. A map has a scale of 1 : 10 000. What distance does 5cm represent on the map? 500m
4. (Level 8) Complete the table: $y \propto x^2$.

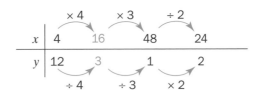

$$\begin{array}{c|cccc} & \times 2 & \times 3 & \times 4 \\ x & 2 & 4 & 12 & 48 \\ \hline y & 3 & 12 & 108 & 1728 \\ & \times 2^2 & \times 3^2 & \times 4^2 \end{array}$$

Answers (inverted): 1. £1.60 2. £30 3. 500m 4.

$$\begin{array}{c|cccc} & \times 2 & \times 3 & \times 4 \\ x & 2 & 4 & 12 & 48 \\ \hline y & 3 & 12 & 108 & 1728 \\ & \times 2^2 & \times 3^2 & \times 4^2 \end{array}$$

Assessment questions

Try the following questions.

(Level 4) **1.** Gill has 3 cards. | 5 | | 7 | | 1 |

(a) Rearrange the cards to make the largest possible number. _751_

(b) What is the smallest number Gill can make with the three cards? _157_

(Level 4) **2.** Some fractions are written on cards. Which fractions are equivalent to $\frac{2}{5}$?

| $\frac{4}{10}$ | $\frac{6}{10}$ | $\frac{10}{25}$ | $\frac{10}{20}$ | $\frac{10}{40}$ | $\frac{8}{20}$ | $\frac{5}{20}$ | $\frac{20}{50}$ |

$\frac{20}{50} \quad \frac{10}{25} \quad \frac{4}{10} \quad \frac{8}{20}$

(Level 5) **3.** Here are some numbered discs: (16) (12) (2) (9) (1) (15) (5)

From the discs write down:
(a) the discs that are prime numbers _2, 5_

(b) the discs that are factors of 12 _1, 2, 12_

(c) the discs that are square numbers. _9, 16_

(Level 5) **4.** The temperature at midnight on one day in December is -12°C. If the temperature rises by 22 degrees by midday, what is the temperature at midday?

_10 °C_

(Level 5) **5.** Evaluate:
(a) $\sqrt{144}$ _12_ (b) 2^3 _8_ (c) $\sqrt[3]{64}$ _____

(Level 6) **6.** A television costing £850 cash is sold by hire purchase. The hire-purchase agreement states the following: **20% deposit of the cash price**
15 instalments of £52 per month

Work out the cost of the television under the hire-purchase agreement. _____

(Level 6) **7.** Put these decimals in order, starting with the smallest.
3.24, 4.16, 4.07, 3.241, 4.105

_____

(Level 6) **8.** A charity ball earns £6320. Three-fifths of the money goes to a children's charity.

How much money is paid to the children's charity? _____

(Level 6) **9.** Work out:
(a) 26.52 + 37.13 (b) 46.21 − 41.235 (c) $\frac{1}{3} + \frac{2}{7}$ (d) $\frac{9}{11} \div \frac{3}{5}$

_____

(Level 6) **10.** Match up the calculations in Column A with the correct answers in Column B.

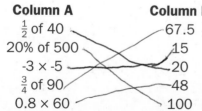

Column A	Column B
$\frac{1}{2}$ of 40	67.5
20% of 500	15
-3 × -5	20
$\frac{3}{4}$ of 90	48
0.8 × 60	100

Assessment questions

Level 6 **11.** A sweater costs £65. In a sale it is reduced by 20%. What is the sale price? _____

Level 6 **12.** In a packet of seeds, the ratio of white flowers to red flowers is 2 : 5. If there are 140 seeds in the packet, how many red flowers would you expect? _____

Level 6 **13.** The fractions, decimals and percentages in each column are equal. Fill in the blank spaces.

Fraction	_____	_____	$\frac{5}{8}$	_____	_____	$\frac{1}{3}$
Decimal	_____	0.35	_____	_____	0.23	_____
Percentage	20%	_____	_____	45%	_____	_____

Level 6 **14.** Sukhvinder wins £20 000 on the lottery. She shares her winnings in the ratio 2 : 3 between her two children. How much does each child receive?

_____

Level 6 **15.** A bike is bought for £85. Two years later it is sold for £62.
Work out the percentage loss.

_____

Level 6 **16.** A supermarket sells 'Superflakes' breakfast cereal in three different-sized packets.

250g 500g 700g
£1.10 £1.95 £2.20

Which packet is the best value for money?
_____

Level 6 **17.** Frances scored 28 out of 62 in a Maths test. What percentage did she get? _____

Level 7 **18.** A clothing shop has a sale. For each day of the sale, prices are reduced by 20% of the prices on the day before. A sweater was priced at £45 on Monday. If the sale starts on Tuesday, how much does Mary pay for the sweater if she buys it on Wednesday?

_____

Level 7 **19.** Matthew invests £6000. Compound interest is paid at 3% per year.
How much does he have at the end of three years? _____

Level 8 **20.** Evaluate the following:

(a) 4^{-1} **(b)** $2^4 \times 2^3$ **(c)** 6^0 **(d)** $16^{\frac{1}{2}}$ **(e)** 3^{-2}

_____

Level 8 **21. (a)** Write six million in standard form. _____
     (b) Evaluate the following:
          (i) $(2 \times 10^6) \times (3 \times 10^4)$ _____ **(ii)** $(1.2 \times 10^{-9}) \div (2 \times 10^{-4})$ _____

Level 8 **22.** Prove that $\frac{4}{9}$ equals $0.\dot{4}$ _____

Level 8 **23.** The price of a washing machine after a 15% reduction is £425.
What was the original price of the washing machine? _____

2 Calculations

Learning Summary

After studying this section you should be able to:

- use a variety of written and mental methods to work out calculations
- use a variety of calculator methods to work out calculations
- use a calculator efficiently and appropriately to perform complex calculations
- approximate and estimate answers to complex calculations

2.1 Written and calculator methods

Addition

When adding integers and decimals, the place values must line up, one on top of the other.

> **Example**
>
> Work out 5279 + 408
>
> Line up the digits first.
>
> $$\begin{array}{r} 5\ 2\ 7\ 9 \\ 4\ 0\ 8\ + \\ \hline 5\ 6\ 8\ 7 \\ 1 \end{array}$$
>
> Add the units then the hundreds, etc.
>
> The 1 is carried here into the tens column.
>
> 5279 + 408
>
>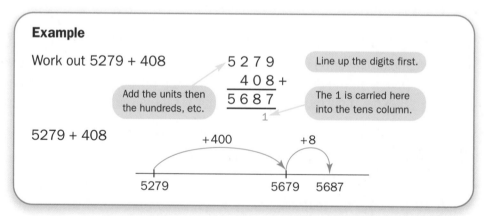

This addition can be checked mentally by using **partitioning** and an empty number line to help.

The same methods can be used when the numbers are decimals.

> **Example**
>
> Work out 127.3 + 9.07
>
> Line up the decimal points.
>
> $$\begin{array}{r} 127.3 \\ 9.07\ + \\ \hline 136.37 \end{array}$$
>
> Checking by partitioning gives:
>
>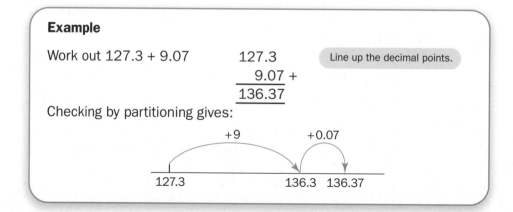

Subtraction

When subtracting integers and decimals, the place values must line up one on top of the other. Subtracting is also known as finding the **difference**.

Compensation can be used to check the answer, by adding or subtracting too much and then compensating.

Example

Work out 2791 − 365

$$
\begin{array}{r}
2\,7\,\overset{8}{9}\,\overset{1}{1} \\
3\,6\,5\, - \\
\hline
2\,4\,2\,6
\end{array}
$$

In the units column 1 − 5 won't work. Borrow 10 from the next column. So the 9 becomes 8 and the 1 becomes 11.

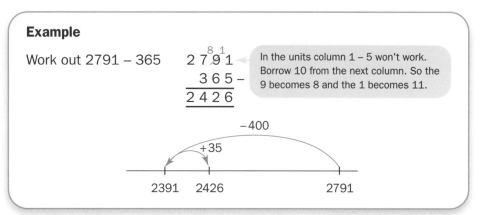

-400

$+35$

2391   2426   2791

Multiplication

Multiplying is much easier if you know the multiplication tables. Using a **grid method** can sometimes help when multiplying.

Example

Work out 6.24 × 8

$$
\begin{array}{r}
6.24 \\
8\, \times \\
\hline
49.92 \\
\scriptstyle 1\ 3
\end{array}
$$

Multiply each of the digits 6, 2, 4 by 8. Start from the right and move to the left.

Alternatively, if a grid method is used:

×	6	0.2	0.04	Answer
8	48	1.6	0.32	49.92

Multiplying two or more numbers together is known as finding the **product**.

Example

Work out 1.89 × 23

This calculation involves long multiplication. This is made easier if we multiply 1.89 × 100 to remove the decimal point.

$$
\begin{array}{r}
189 \\
23\, \times \\
\hline
567 \\
3780 \\
\hline
4347
\end{array}
$$

189 × 3

189 × 20

The answer now needs to be divided by 100 because we multiplied by 100 originally.

Answer = 4347 ÷ 100 = 43.47

Alternatively, using a grid method gives:

	100	80	9
20	2000	1600	180
3	300	240	27

$$
\begin{array}{r}
3780 \\
567\, + \\
\hline
4347
\end{array}
$$

Division

Care must be taken when carrying out long and short division that important zeros are not missed out.

> The method of 'chunking' can be used when dividing. Always try to estimate the answer to your division.

Example

A bar of chocolate costs 74p. Tracey has £9.82 to spend. What is the maximum number of bars Tracey can buy? How much change does she have left?

$$
\begin{array}{r}
13 \\
74\overline{)98\,2} \\
74\,- \\
\hline
24\,2 \\
22\,2\,- \\
\hline
20
\end{array}
$$
or
$$
\begin{array}{r}
74\overline{)98\,2} \\
74\,0\,- \quad 74 \times 10 \\
\hline
24\,2 \\
22\,2\,- \quad 74 \times 3 \\
\hline
20
\end{array}
$$

Tracey can buy 13 bars and has 20p left over.

Answer = 10 + 3
= 13 bars
and 20p left over.

In this example, the 74 is the **divisor**, the 13 is the **quotient** and the **remainder** is 20p.

When dividing by decimals, it is useful to change to an equivalent calculation that does not have a decimal divisor.

For example:
372.8 ÷ 0.4 is equivalent to 3728 ÷ 4
527.1 ÷ 0.02 is equivalent to 52710 ÷ 2

Order of operations

BIDMAS is a made-up word that helps you to remember the order in which calculations take place.

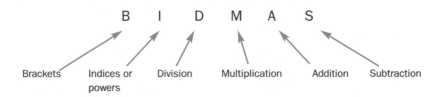

B   I   D   M   A   S

Brackets   Indices or powers   Division   Multiplication   Addition   Subtraction

> This order of operations is also used in algebra.

This means that brackets are worked out first and, in the absence of brackets, division and multiplication are done before addition and subtraction.

For example:
- $(3 + 4) \times 5 = 35$ ← The brackets are carried out first.
- $5^2 - (2 \times 3) = 25 - 6 = 19$
- $6 + 3 \times 2 = 12$ ← The multiplication is carried out first.

Important calculator keys

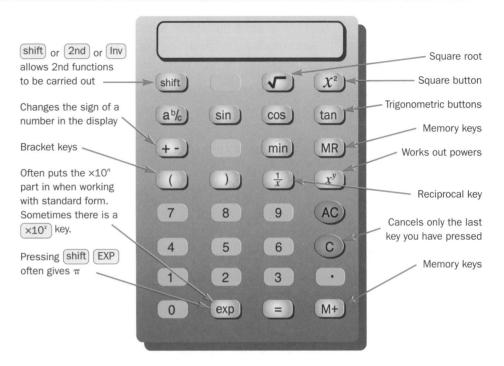

shift or 2nd or Inv allows 2nd functions to be carried out

Changes the sign of a number in the display

Bracket keys

Often puts the ×10ⁿ part in when working with standard form. Sometimes there is a ×10ˣ key.

Pressing shift EXP often gives π

Square root

Square button

Trigonometric buttons

Memory keys

Works out powers

Reciprocal key

Cancels only the last key you have pressed

Memory keys

This is an example of a calculator just to show you some of the important calculator keys. Make sure you know how your calculator works.

For example:
$$\frac{15 \times 10 + 46}{9.3 \times 2.1} = 10.04 \text{ (2 d.p.)}$$

This may be keyed in as:

(15 × 10 + 46) ÷ (9.3 × 2.1) =

The above calculation can also be done using the memory keys.
Try writing down the key sequence for yourself.

Calculating powers and reciprocals

Level 7 y^x , x^y or $x^\square$ are used to calculate powers such as 2^7.

Use the power key on the calculator to work out 2^7:

Keying in gives 2 x^y 7 = (check your answer is 128).

$\frac{1}{x}$ is the **reciprocal** key on the calculator. It is used to calculate the reciprocal of a number.

For example:
- $9^{\frac{1}{3}} \times 4^5 = 2130$ (to the nearest whole number)
- The reciprocal of $0.3 = 3.\dot{3}$

Standard form and the calculator

(Level 8) To key a number in standard form into the calculator, use the [EXP] key. (Some calculators use [EE] or [×10^x]. Check your calculator.)

For example:

- 6.23 × 10^6 can be keyed in as [6] [.] [2] [3] [EXP] [6]
- 4.93 × 10^{-5} can be keyed in as [4] [.] [9] [3] [EXP] [+/−] [5]

> Make sure you know how your calculator works.

Some calculators do not show standard form correctly on the display:

7.632^7 means 7.632 × 10^7

4.2^{-09} means 4.2 × 10^{-9}

It is important to put in the ×10 part when you write your answer.

Interpreting the calculator display

When calculations involve money, the following points need to be remembered:

- A display of 4.2 means £4.20 (four pounds twenty pence).
- A display of 3.07 means £3.07 (three pounds and seven pence).
- A display of 0.64 means £0.64 or 64 pence.
- A display of 6.2934 means £6.29, i.e. it has to be rounded to 2 d.p.

Progress Check

1. Work out the following, without using a calculator.
   (a) 27.4 × 32
   (b) 3762 ÷ 3
   (c) 690 ÷ 15
   (d) 3729 × 46
   (e) 237.2 ÷ 0.8

2. Work out the following on your calculator.
   (a) $\dfrac{27.1 \times 6.4}{9.3 + 2.7}$ (b) $\dfrac{(9.3)^4}{2.7 \times 3.6}$

   (c) $\sqrt{\dfrac{25^2}{4\pi}}$ (d) $\dfrac{5}{9}(25 - 10)$

3. Without using a calculator, which is the correct answer?
   (a) 2 + 3 × 7   A 35   B 23
   (b) 4 − 1 × 5   A 15   B -1
   (c) (9 + 1)^2 × 4   A 1600   B 400

3. (a) **B** 23 (b) **B** -1 (c) **B** 400
2. (a) 14.45 (2 d.p.) (b) 769.6 (1 d.p.) (c) 7.052 (3 d.p.) (d) $8\frac{1}{3}$ or 8.3
1. (a) 876.8 (b) 1254 (c) 46 (d) 171 534 (e) 296.5

2.2 Rounding and estimating

Rounding numbers

Large numbers are often **approximated** to the nearest ten, hundred or thousand to make them easier to work with.

Rounding to the nearest ten

Look at the digit in the units column. If it is less than 5, round down. If it is 5 or more, round up.

Example

568 people attended a concert. Round this to the nearest ten.

There is an 8 in the units column, so round up to 570. 568 is 570 to the nearest ten.

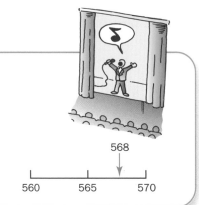

568

560   565   570

Rounding to the nearest hundred

Look at the digit in the tens column. If it is less than 5, round down. If it is 5 or more, round up.

Example

In May, 2650 people went to the zoo. Round this to the nearest hundred.

Since there is a 5 in the tens column, we round up to 2700. 2650 is 2700 to the nearest hundred.

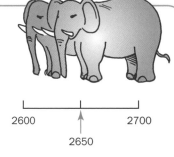

2600   2700

2650

Rounding to the nearest thousand

Look at the digits in the hundreds column. The same rules apply as before.

Example

Round 16 420 to the nearest thousand.

There is a 4 in the hundreds column, so round down to 16 000.

16 420 is 16 000 to the nearest thousand.

16 420

16 000   16 500   17 000

Similar methods can be used to estimate any number to any power of 10.

Newspaper reports often use rounded numbers. Here 14 725 437 has been rounded to the nearest million.

DAILY NEWS
15 MILLION TOURISTS VISIT LONDON
14,725,437 people

Decimal places (d.p.)

It is sometimes useful to round decimals to the nearest whole number or to a specified number of decimal places.

The same rules of rounding shown on page 37 are used.

Key Point

To round to the nearest whole number, look at the number in the first decimal place:
- If it is 5 or more, round the units up to the next whole number.
- If it is less than 5, the units stay the same.

Example

Round to the nearest whole number:
(a) 12.3 = 12 to the nearest whole number
(b) 7.9 = 8 to the nearest whole number.

Key Point

To round to the nearest tenth (or to 1 decimal place), look at the number in the second decimal place:
- If it is 5 or more, round the first decimal place up to the next tenth.
- If it is less than 5, the first decimal place remains the same.

Example

Round these numbers to 1 decimal place:
(a) 9.45 = 9.5 (1 d.p.)
(b) 12.57 = 12.6 (1 d.p.)

6 6.5 7 7.5 8 8.5 9 9.5

A similar method can be used when rounding any number to a particular number of decimal places.

Here are some more examples:
- 16.59 = 16.6 (1 d.p.)
- 12.3642 = 12.364 (3 d.p.)
- 8.435 = 8.44 (2 d.p.)

Significant figures (s.f. or sig. fig.)

(Level 7) The rule for rounding to a given number of significant figures is the same as for decimal places: if the next digit is 5 or more, round up.

The first **significant** figure is the **first digit** that is not a **zero**. The 2nd, 3rd, 4th ... significant figures follow on after the first digit. They may or may not be zero.

For example:

7.021 has 4 s.f.

0.003 706 has 4 s.f.

1st 2nd 3rd 4th   1st 2nd 3rd 4th

It is important that, when rounding, the place value is not changed.

Here are some examples of rounding to a certain number of significant figures:

Number	to 3 s.f.	to 2 s.f.	to 1 s.f.
4.207	4.21	4.2	4
4379	4380	4400	4000
0.006 209	0.006 21	0.0062	0.006

Key Point

After rounding, the end zeros must be filled in. For example, 4380 = 4400 to 2 s.f. (not 44). No extra zeros should be put in after the decimal point. For example, 0.013 = 0.01 to 1 s.f., not 0.010

Possible error of half a unit when rounding

Key Point

Level 7 If a measurement has been rounded, the actual measurement lies within a maximum of half a unit of that amount. It can be half a unit bigger or smaller.

There are two types of measurement: discrete and continuous.

Discrete measures

Discrete measures are quantities that can be counted, such as people.

For example, a school has 1400 pupils to 2 s.f. (i.e. the nearest 100). The actual figure could be anything from 1350 to 1449.

Continuous measures

Continuous measures are measurements that have been made by using a measuring instrument, such as a person's height. Continuous measures are not exact.

For example, Nigel weighs 72kg to the nearest kg. His actual weight could be anywhere between 71.5kg and 72.5kg.

```
              − 0.5      + 0.5
        |____|____|____|____|____|
      71kg  71.5kg  72kg  72.5kg  73kg
```

These two values are the limits of Nigel's weight.

If w represents weight, then

$$71.5 \leq w < 72.5$$

This is the **lower limit** of Nigel's weight (sometimes known as the **lower bound**.) Anything below 71.5 would be recorded as 71kg.

This is the **upper limit** (**upper bound**) of Nigel's weight. Anything from 72.5 upwards would be read as 73kg.

Example

The length of a seedling is measured as 3.7cm to the nearest tenth of a centimetre. What are the upper and lower limits of the length?

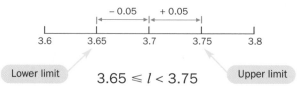

Lower limit $3.65 \leqslant l < 3.75$ Upper limit

Rounding sensibly in calculations

When solving problems the answers should be rounded sensibly. It is wise to go back and check the context of the question.

Examples

(a) Mr Singh organised a trip to the theatre for 420 students and 10 teachers. If a coach can seat 53 people, how many coaches did he need?

$430 \div 53 = 8.11$ coaches
9 coaches are needed.

> Obviously, not everybody can get on 8 coaches ($8 \times 53 = 424$) so we need to round up to 9 coaches.

(b) Work out 95.26×6.39

$95.26 \times 6.39 = 608.7114$
$\qquad\qquad\quad = 608.71$ (2 d.p.)

> The answer is rounded to 2 d.p. because the values in the question are to 2 d.p.

(c) James has £9.37. He divides it equally between 5 people. How much does each person receive?

£9.37 $\div$ 5 = £1.874
$\qquad\quad = $ £1.87

> This is rounded to 2 d.p. because it involves money.

Checking calculations

Key Point	A calculation can be checked by carrying out the **inverse** operation.

For example:

- $106 \times 3 = 318$
  Inverse: $318 \div 3 = 106$
  or $\qquad 318 \div 106 = 3$

  $106 \xrightarrow{\times 3} 318$ $\xleftarrow{\div 3}$

- $\sqrt{5} = 2.236\,067\,977$
  Inverse: $(2.236\,067\,977)^2 = 5$

  $5 \xrightarrow{\sqrt{}} 2.236\,067\,977$ $\xleftarrow{x^2}$

- 692×4 $\qquad$ Check with $(700 - 8) \times 4 = 2800 - 32$
  $= 2768$ $\qquad\qquad\qquad\qquad\qquad\qquad = 2768$

> A calculation can also be checked by carrying out an **equivalent** calculation.

Estimating

Estimating is a good way of checking answers. Estimating can help you to decide whether an answer is the **right order of magnitude**, which means 'about the right size'.

When estimating:
- round the numbers to 'easy' numbers, usually 1 or 2 significant figures
- work out the estimate using these 'easy' numbers
- use the symbol $\approx$ which means '**approximately equal to**'.

Key Point

For multiplying or dividing, never approximate a number to zero. Use 0.1, 0.01, 0.001, etc.

> **Examples**
>
> **(a)** Estimate the following calculations:
>
> **(i)** $8.93 \times 25.09 \approx 10 \times 25 = 250$
>
> **(ii)** $(6.29)^2 \approx 6^2 = 36$
>
> **(iii)** $\dfrac{296 \times 52.1}{9.72 \times 1.14} \approx \dfrac{300 \times 50}{10 \times 1} = \dfrac{15\,000}{10} = 1500$
>
> **(iv)** $0.096 \times 79.2 \approx 0.1 \times 80 = 8$
>
> **(b)** Jack does the calculation $\dfrac{9.6 \times 103}{(2.9)^2}$
>
>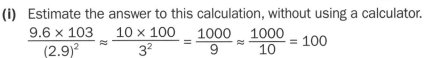
>
> **(i)** Estimate the answer to this calculation, without using a calculator.
> $$\frac{9.6 \times 103}{(2.9)^2} \approx \frac{10 \times 100}{3^2} = \frac{1000}{9} \approx \frac{1000}{10} = 100$$
>
> **(ii)** Jack's answer is 1175.7. Is this the right order of magnitude?
>
> Jack's answer is not the right order of magnitude. It is 10 times too big.

Remember that 'right order of magnitude' means 'about the right size'.

There are different ways of finding an approximate answer.

For example:
$8.93 \times 25.09 \approx 10 \times 25 = 250$
$\qquad\qquad\quad$ or $9 \times 25 = 225$

In this case, 9×25 is a closer approximation.

You need to be able to recognise what makes a 'good approximation'.

Key Point	When adding and subtracting, very small numbers may be approximated to zero.

Examples

Estimate the following calculations:
(a) 109.2 + 0.0002

$\approx 110 + 0 = 110$

(b) 63.87 − 0.01

$\approx 64 − 0 = 64$

Progress Check

1. Round the following numbers to the nearest ten.
   (a) 268 **(b)** 1273 **(c)** 42 956 **(d)** 2385
2. Round the following numbers to 2 decimal places.
   (a) 47.365 **(b)** 21.429 **(c)** 15.3725
3. (Level 7) Round the following numbers to 2 significant figures.
   (a) 1247 **(b)** 0.003 729
4. Paint is sold in 8-litre tins. Sandra needs 27 litres of paint. How many tins must she buy?
5. (Level 7) Estimate the answers to the following:
   (a) $\dfrac{(29.4)^2 + 106}{2.2 \times 5.1}$ **(b)** $\dfrac{294 + 101}{2.1 \times 5.2}$

5. (a) 100 (b) 40
4. 4 tins
3. (a) 1200 (b) 0.0037
2. (a) 47.37 (b) 21.43 (c) 15.37
1. (a) 270 (b) 1270 (c) 42 960 (d) 2390

Assessment questions

Try the following questions.

(Level 4) 1. The following table shows the different sizes of some schools. Complete the table by rounding to the nearest 10 and 100.

School	Number of pupils	Number of pupils to nearest	
		10	100
Appletown	1522	_____	_____
Beetown	1306	_____	_____
Nortown	2714	_____	_____
Duncetown	456	_____	_____

(Level 4) 2. There are 7 rows of cabbages. Altogether there are 315 cabbages.
How many cabbages are there in each row? _____

(Level 5) 3. Work out:
    (a) 27.43 + 16.82 _____ **(b)** 137.42 − 102.63 _____
    (c) 5.2 × 4.3 _____ **(d)** 13.5 ÷ 3 _____

(Level 5) 4. A jar of coffee costs £2.45. Work out the cost of 18 jars. _____

(Level 5) 5. Sophie is holding a conference. She needs 975 biscuits. One packet holds 37 biscuits.
    (a) How many packets of biscuits must Sophie buy? _____
    (b) How many spare biscuits will she have? _____
    (c) Each packet of biscuits costs 84p. How much will Sophie spend on biscuits? _____

(Level 5) 6. How many boxes of 45 nails can be filled from 340 nails? _____

(Level 5) 7. James and Lucy carry out this calculation: 5 + 3 × 7
James says the answer is 56. Lucy disagrees and says the answer is 26. Who is correct?
(Give a reason for your answer.)

_____

(Level 5) 8. Fill in the missing numbers:

    (a) (____ × 4) ÷ 8 = 5   **(b)** ____^{2} × 4 = 16

(Level 5) 9. Mr Johnson tries to work out the answer to 292 × 42. He works it out as 1226.4, but he thinks he has made a mistake.
    (a) Make a rough estimate of 292 × 42. _____
    (b) Compare your estimate with Mr Johnson's answer. Do you think he made a mistake? If so, can you explain it?

_____

    (c) What is the exact answer to 292 × 42? _____

(Level 5) 10. Sue worked out £4.24 + 82p on a calculator. If the display showed 86.24, what did Sue do wrong when she keyed in the calculation? _____

(Level 6) 11. Fill in the gaps:

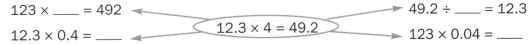

    123 × ____ = 492   49.2 ÷ ____ = 12.3
    12.3 × 0.4 = ____   12.3 × 4 = 49.2   123 × 0.04 = ____

Assessment questions

Level 7 **12.** Complete the table below.

Number	2 decimal places	2 significant figures	1 significant figure
272.438			
41.271			
1.3728			
147.525			

Level 7 **13.** Use a calculator to work out the following: 🖩

(a) $\dfrac{8.2 - 3.1}{8.2 + 3.1}$ _____ (b) $4 \times (7.32)^2$ _____

(c) $\dfrac{55.62 \times 7.31}{1.09 \times (7.2 - 4.3)}$ _____ (d) $\{(4.2)^2 + (6.3 - 2.471)\}^2$ _____

(e) $\dfrac{5 \times \sqrt{(4.2^2 + 8^2)}}{3}$ _____

Level 7 **14.** Erin worked out $\dfrac{5.79 + 3.27}{6.3^2 \times 4}$ on her calculator. She got 6.12 (2 d.p.)

(a) Work out the calculation. 🖩 _____

(b) Explain the mistake Erin made in obtaining her answer.

_____

Level 7 **15.** If the reciprocal of 1.145 is 0.873 362 445, what is the reciprocal of 0.873 362 445? Explain your answer.

_____

Level 7 **16.** The population of Greece is 25 million to the nearest million. What is:

(a) the smallest possible population? _____

(b) the greatest possible population? _____

Level 7 **17.** The distance, d, from London to Manchester is 340km, to the nearest km. Write down:

(a) the least possible distance _____

(b) the greatest possible distance. _____

Level 8 **18.** Look at the following cards:

1.26×10^9	1.5×10^{-8}	7.31×10^{-9}	6×10^4
A	B	C	D

Write these numbers, correct to 3 s.f., in standard index form: 🖩

(a) A × B _____ (b) C ÷ D _____

(c) B + C _____ (d) $C^2 \times A$ _____

Algebra

Equations, formulae and identities			Studied	Revised	Assessment questions
3.1	Symbols and formulae	– Using letter symbols – Know the words – Collecting like terms – Multiplying letters, numbers and brackets – Factorising – Factorising quadratic expressions – Algebraic fractions – Indices and algebra – Writing formulae – Substituting values into formulae and expressions – Rearranging formulae			
3.2	Equations and inequalities	– Linear equations – Using equations to solve problems – Simultaneous linear equations – Solving cubic equations by trial and improvement – Inequalities – Graphs of inequalities			

Sequences, functions and graphs			Studied	Revised	Assessment questions
4.1	Sequences and functions	– Sequences – Finding the nth term of a linear sequence – Finding the nth term of a quadratic sequence – Fraction sequences – Generating sequences from practical examples – Function machines and mapping			
4.2	Graphs of functions	– Coordinates – Straight-line graphs – Finding the gradient of a straight line – Graphs that are not straight lines			
4.3	Interpreting graphical information	– Using linear graphs – Conversion graphs – Distance-time graphs – Matching graphs to real-life situations			

3 Equations, formulae and identities

Learning Summary

After studying this section you should be able to:

- construct and use formulae from mathematics and other subjects
- manipulate algebraic formulae, equations and expressions
- construct and solve linear equations
- solve simultaneous linear equations in two variables
- solve inequalities and find the solution set

3.1 Symbols and formulae

Key Point

In algebra we use letters as symbols. The letters represent:
- unknown numbers in an **equation**
- **variables** in a **formula**, which can take many values, e.g. $V = IR$
- numbers in an **identity**, which can take any values, e.g.
  $3(x + 2) \equiv 3x + 6$, for any value of x

A **term** is a number or a letter, or a combination of both multiplied together. Terms are separated by + and − signs. Each term has a + or − sign attached to the front of it.

For example:

$$5ab + 2c - 3c^2 + 5$$

Invisible + sign ab term c term c^2 term   Number term

A collection of terms is known as an **expression**.

Using letter symbols

There are several rules to follow when writing expressions:
- $a + a + a$ is written as $3a$
- $a \times b$ is written as ab
- $a \times 3 \times b$ is written as $3ab$ *Here the number is written first and the letters are put in alphabetical order.*
- $b \times b$ is written as b^2, which is not the same as $2b$
- $b \times b \times b$ is written as b^3, which is not the same as $3b$
- $n \times n \times 3$ is written as $3n^2$, not $(3n)^2$
- $a \times (b + c)$ is written as $a(b + c)$
- $(a + b) \div c$ is written as $\frac{(a + b)}{c}$

Example

In a game John has r counters. Write down the number of counters each person has using r.
(a) Carol has twice as many counters as John. Carol has $2r$.
(b) Vali has 12 fewer than John. Vali has $r - 12$.
(c) Stuart has half as many as John. Stuart has $r \div 2 = \dfrac{r}{2}$.
(d) Hilary has 5 fewer than Carol. Hilary has $2r - 5$.

Know the words

The following words are used in algebra; some have already been mentioned.
- **Expression** – any arrangement of letter symbols and numbers, e.g. $2a + 3b - 4$.
- **Formula** – connects two expressions containing variables, the value of one variable depending on the values of the others. It must have an equals sign, e.g. $v = u + at$. When the values of u, a and t are known, the value of v can be found.
- **Equation** – connects two expressions involving definite unknown values. It must have an equals sign, e.g. $x + 2 = 5$.
- **Identity** – connects expressions involving unspecified numbers. An identity always remains true, no matter what numerical values replace the letter symbols. It has an '$\equiv$' sign, e.g. $3(x + 2) \equiv 3x + 6$. This is true no matter what values of x are used.
- **Function** – a relationship between two sets of values, such that a value from the first set maps onto a unique value in the second set, e.g. $y = 4x + 2$. For any value of x, the value of y can be calculated.

Collecting like terms

Key Point

Expressions can be **simplified** by collecting like terms. Like terms have the same letters and powers.

Examples

(a) Simplify:
    (i) $3a + 4a = 7a$
    (ii) $6a + 2b$ cannot be simplified, since there are no like terms.
    (iii) $3n + 2n - 4n = n$
    (iv) $5a + 4b + 3a - 6b = 8a - 2b$ Add the a terms then the b terms.

The minus is part of the $6b$.

Remember to put the sign between the terms, i.e. $8a - 2b$ not $8a\ 2b$.

    (v) $5xy + 2yx = 7xy$, since xy is the same as yx
    (vi) $5n^2 + 2n + 3n^2 = 8n^2 + 2n$

(b) The expression in each cell is made by adding the expressions in the two cells beneath it. Fill in the missing expressions, writing each expression as simply as possible.

?

$5u + 3p$	$3p - 2u$

?	$3p$	$-2u$

$3u + 6p$ because $5u + 3p + 3p - 2u$
$= 3u + 6p$

This would be $5u$ so that $5u + 3p$ gives the expression above.

Multiplying letters, numbers and brackets

Algebraic expressions that are multiplied together can often be **simplified**, e.g. $5a \times 2b = 10ab$.

When multiplying expressions, multiply the numbers together, then the letters.

Example

Simplify these expressions:

(a) $3a \times 4b = 3 \times 4 \times a \times b = 12ab$

(b) $5a \times 3b \times 2c = 5 \times 3 \times 2 \times a \times b \times c = 30abc$

(c) $2a \times 3a = 2 \times 3 \times a \times a = 6a^2$ Remember $a \times a = a^2$

Key Point

When multiplying out single and double brackets, use the same rules as for operations with numbers.

Multiplying out single brackets

Everything inside the bracket must be multiplied by everything outside the bracket. **Partitioning** can be used.

Expand just means multiply out the brackets.

Examples

Expand the following:

(a) $2(a + b)$
$= 2 \times a + 2 \times b$
$= 2a + 2b$

	a	b
2	$2 \times a$	$2 \times b$

(b) $a(b + c)$
$= a \times b + a \times c$
$= ab + ac$

	b	c
a	$a \times b$	$a \times c$

(c) $3(a + 2)$
$= 3 \times a + 3 \times 2$
$= 3a + 6$

(d) $a(2a + 3b)$
$= a \times 2a + a \times 3b$
$= 2a^2 + 3ab$

Key Point

If the term outside the bracket is **negative**, all the signs of the terms inside the brackets are changed when multiplying out.

Examples

Expand the following:

(a) $-3(a + b) = -3a - 3b$

(b) $-(a - b) = -a + b$ Remember $-(a - b)$ means $-1 \times (a - b)$

(c) $-a(a - b) = -a^2 + ab$

To **simplify** expressions, expand the brackets first and then collect like terms.

Examples

Expand and simplify the following:

(a) $2(a + 3) + 3(a + 1)$
$= 2a + 6 + 3a + 3$
$= 5a + 9$

(b) $5(a + b) - 2(a + 2b)$
$= 5a + 5b - 2a - 4b$
$= 3a + b$

Multiplying out two brackets

(Level 7) Each term in the first bracket is multiplied with each term in the second bracket. A grid method can be used to help when multiplying out two brackets.

Examples

Expand and simplify the following:

(a) $(x + 2)(x + 4)$ $= x(x + 4) + 2(x + 4)$ or
$= x^2 + 4x + 2x + 8$
$= x^2 + 6x + 8$

	x	4
x	x^2	$4x$
2	$2x$	8

$= x^2 + 4x + 2x + 8$
$= x^2 + 6x + 8$

> A common error is to think that $(x - 3)^2$ means $x^2(-3)^2 = x^2 + 9$. It does not!

(b) $(x - 3)^2 = (x - 3)(x - 3)$
$= x(x - 3) - 3(x - 3)$ or
$= x^2 - 3x - 3x + 9$
$= x^2 - 6x + 9$

	x	-3
x	x^2	$-3x$
-3	$-3x$	$+9$

$= x^2 - 3x - 3x + 9$
$= x^2 - 6x + 9$

> This identity is very important. It is known as the 'difference of two squares'.

(c) (Level 8) $(x - a)(x + a) = x(x + a) - a(x + a)$
$= x^2 + ax - ax - a^2$
$= x^2 - a^2$

Factorising

Factorising is the reverse of **expanding brackets**. An expression is put into brackets by taking out common factors.

For example, to factorise $xy + 4y$:
- recognise that y is a factor of each term
- take out the common factor
- the expression is completed inside the bracket, so that the result is equivalent to $xy + 4y$ when multiplied out.

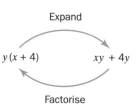

Expand

$y(x + 4)$ $xy + 4y$

Factorise

Here are some more examples:
$$8x - 16 = 8(x - 2)$$
$$3x + 18 = 3(x + 6)$$
$$5x^2 + x = x(5x + 1)$$
$$4x^2 + 8x = 4x(x + 2)$$
$$x^3 + 2x^2 + 4x = x(x^2 + 2x + 4)$$

Factorising quadratic expressions

(Level 8) You need to be able to factorise quadratic expressions into a pair of linear brackets.

Examples

Factorise the following:

(a) $x^2 + 7x + 10$
$$x^2 + 7x + 10 = (x \pm a)(x \pm b)$$
$$x^2 + 7x + 10 = (x + 5)(x + 2)$$

> These values multiply to give 10 and add to make 7.
> $5 \times 2 = 10$ and $5 + 2 = 7$

(b) $x^2 - 4x + 3$
$$x^2 - 4x + 3 = (x - 1)(x - 3)$$

> Since $-1 \times -3 = 3$ and $-1 - 3 = -4$

(c) $x^2 + 6x - 7$
$$x^2 + 6x - 7 = (x + 7)(x - 1)$$

> Since $7 \times -1 = -7$ and $7 - 1 = 6$

(d) $x^2 - 16$
$$x^2 - 16 = (x + 4)(x - 4)$$

> This is known as the difference of two squares.

Key Point

In general, $x^2 - a^2 = (x + a)(x - a)$

Algebraic fractions

You need to be able to add simple algebraic fractions. The same rules that apply to fractions in arithmetic can be used here.

> Algebra is generalised arithmetic so we can use the same methods.

Example

Simplify the following:

(a) $\dfrac{a}{4} + \dfrac{b}{2} = \dfrac{a + 2b}{4}$

> Make $\dfrac{b}{2}$ into its equivalent fraction with a denominator of 4, then add the numerators.

(b) (Level 7) $\dfrac{a}{n} + \dfrac{c}{m} = \dfrac{am}{mn} + \dfrac{cn}{mn} = \dfrac{am + cn}{mn}$

> mn is the common denominator.

Indices and algebra

Key Point

(Level 8) The laws of indices that apply to numbers also apply to algebra. The index laws are:

- $a^n \times a^m = a^{n+m}$
- $a^n \div a^m = a^{n-m}$
- $(a^n)^m = a^{n \times m}$
- $a^0 = 1$

- $a^{-n} = \dfrac{1}{a^n}$
- $a^{\frac{1}{n}} = \sqrt[n]{a}$
- $a^1 = a$

Examples

Simplify the following:

Note the numbers are multiplied...

(a) $3x^5 \times 4x^3 = 12x^8$

...but powers of the same letter are added.

(b) $15a^{14} \div 3a^{10} = 5a^4$

(c) $(7x^3)^2 = 49x^6$

(d) $x^0 = 1$

(e) $\dfrac{12a^2b^3}{4a^3b} = \dfrac{3b^2}{a} = 3a^{-1}b^2$

(f) $2x^{-3} = \dfrac{2}{x^3}$

(g) $(2x)^{-3} = \dfrac{1}{(2x)^3} = \dfrac{1}{8x^3}$

Writing formulae

A formula can be constructed from some information you are given or from a diagram.

Example

A pattern is made up of blue and yellow tiles.

Pattern number 1   Pattern number 2   Pattern number 3

Make sure there is an = sign in the formula. The $4n$ is the 4 lots of blue tiles. The + 1 is the yellow tile in the middle.

(a) How many blue tiles will there be in pattern number 4?
Drawing the diagram, there are 16 blue tiles.

(b) Write down the formula for finding the number of tiles (t) in pattern number, n.
Number of tiles = $4 \times n + 1$
$$t = 4n + 1$$

Pattern number 4

(c) How many tiles will be used in pattern number 12?
In this case, $n = 12$

$n = 12$ is substituted into the formula.

$t = 4 \times 12 + 1$
$t = 48 + 1$
$t = 49$

Substituting values into formulae and expressions

Replacing a letter with a number is called **substitution**. When substituting, write out the expression first and then replace the letters with the values given.

Work out the values on your calculator. Use bracket keys where possible and pay attention to the **order of operations**.

Examples

(a) Using $a = 2$, $b = 4.1$, $c = -3$ and $d = 5.25$, find the values of these expressions, giving your answers to 1 decimal place.

(i) $\dfrac{a + b}{2} = \dfrac{2 + 4.1}{2} = \dfrac{6.1}{2} = 3.05 = 3.1$ (1 d.p.)

(ii) $\dfrac{a^2 + 2b}{4} = \dfrac{2^2 + 2 \times 4.1}{4} = \dfrac{4 + 8.2}{4} = \dfrac{12.2}{4} = 3.1$ (1 d.p.)

(iii) $\dfrac{a + 2c}{a - d} = \dfrac{2 + 2 \times -3}{2 - 5.25} = \dfrac{-4}{-3.25} = 1.2$ (1 d.p.)

(iv) $\dfrac{3b^2(d - 4)}{2a} = \dfrac{3 \times 4.1^2(5.25 - 4)}{2 \times 2} = \dfrac{50.43(1.25)}{4} = 15.8$ (1 d.p.)

(b) (Level 8) The formula $F = \frac{9}{5}C + 32$ is used to change temperature in degrees centigrade (C) to temperature in degrees Fahrenheit (F). If $C = 20$, find the value of F.

$F = \frac{9}{5}C + 32$

$F = \frac{9}{5} \times 20 + 32$

$F = 68$ degrees

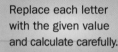
Replace each letter with the given value and calculate carefully.

Rearranging formulae

Key Point

The **subject** of a formula is the letter that appears on its own on one side of the formula.

Inverse operations can be used to change the subject.

Examples

(a) Make R the subject of the formula $V = IR$

$V = IR$

$\dfrac{V}{I} = R$ or $R = \dfrac{V}{I}$ ← Divide both sides by I.

(b) (Level 8) Make r the subject of the formula $V = \pi r^2 h$

$V = \pi r^2 h$

$\dfrac{V}{\pi h} = r^2$ ← Divide both sides by πh.

$\sqrt{\dfrac{V}{\pi h}} = r$ ← Square root both sides.

or $r = \sqrt{\dfrac{V}{\pi h}}$

(c) (Level 8) Make l the subject of the formula $T = 2\pi \sqrt{\dfrac{l}{g}}$

$T = 2\pi \sqrt{\dfrac{l}{g}}$

$\dfrac{T}{2\pi} = \sqrt{\dfrac{l}{g}}$ ← Divide both sides by 2π.

$\left(\dfrac{T}{2\pi}\right)^2 = \dfrac{l}{g}$ ← Square both sides.

$\left(\dfrac{T}{2\pi}\right)^2 \times g = l$ ← Multiply both sides by g.

$l = \left(\dfrac{T}{2\pi}\right)^2 g$ or $l = \dfrac{T^2 g}{4\pi^2}$

Progress Check

1 Simplify these expressions.
   (a) $4(x - 2) + 3(x - 1)$ **(b)** $(n + 1)^2 - 2(n + 2)$

2 Multiply out and simplify:
   (a) $(a - b)^2$ **(b)** $(x - 4)(x + 3)$ **(c)** $(2a + 3)(2a - 1)$

3 To cook a chicken, allow 20 minutes per $\frac{1}{2}$ kg and another 20 minutes. A chicken weighs p kg. Write an expression to show the number of minutes, x, to cook the chicken.

4 The formula for the perimeter P of a rectangle of length l and width w is $P = 2(l + w)$.
   Calculate the width of a rectangle if $P = 60$ and $l = 20$.

5 Make C the subject of the formula $F = \dfrac{9C}{5} + 32$

6 (Level 7) Work out $\dfrac{a}{3} + \dfrac{b}{4}$

7 (Level 8) Simplify:
   (a) $2a^4 \times a^6$ **(b)** $12a^5 \div 2a$ **(c)** $\dfrac{12a^4 b^2}{3ab}$ **(d)** $(8a^2)^2$ **(e)** $(4a^2)^2$

8 (Level 8) Factorise:
   (a) $x^2 + 8x + 15$ **(b)** $x^2 + 3x - 10$ **(c)** $x^2 - 25$

1. (a) $7x - 11$ (b) $n^2 - 3$
2. (a) $a^2 - 2ab + b^2$ (b) $x^2 - x - 12$ (c) $4a^2 + 4a - 3$
3. $x = 40p + 20$
4. $w = 10$
5. $C = \frac{5}{9}(F - 32)$
6. $\dfrac{4a + 3b}{12}$
7. (a) $2a^{10}$ (b) $6a^4$ (c) $4a^3 b$ (d) $64a^4$ (e) $\frac{a^4}{16}$ or $16a^4$
8. (a) $(x + 3)(x + 5)$ (b) $(x + 5)(x - 2)$ (c) $(x + 5)(x - 5)$

3.2 Equations and inequalities

Linear equations

An **equation** has two parts separated by an equals sign. When working out an unknown value in an equation, the **balance method** is usually used; that is, whatever is done to one side of an equation must be done to the other.

Always do the same operation to both sides of the equation.

Examples

Solve the following:

(a) $n - 4 = 6$
$n = 6 + 4$ ← Add 4 to both sides.
$n = 10$

(b) $5n = 20$
$n = \dfrac{20}{5}$ ← Divide both sides by 5.
$n = 4$

(c) $n + 3 = 10$
$n = 10 - 3$ ← Subtract 3 from both sides.
$n = 7$

(d) $\dfrac{n}{2} = 8$
$n = 8 \times 2$ ← Multiply both sides by 2.
$n = 16$

Some equations are of the form $ax + b = c$. These equations involve several steps.

Examples

Solve the following:

(a) $2n - 5 = 11$
$2n = 11 + 5$ ← Add 5 to both sides.
$2n = 16$
$n = \dfrac{16}{2}$ ← Divide both sides by 2.
$n = 8$

(b) $\dfrac{n}{4} + 1 = 3$
$\dfrac{n}{4} = 3 - 1$
$\dfrac{n}{4} = 2$
$n = 2 \times 4$ ← Multiply both sides by 4.
$n = 8$

Some equations are more complicated and have the unknown values on both sides of the equation. These equations are of the form $ax + b = cx + d$. The trick with this type of equation is to get the unknown values together on one side of the equals sign and the numbers on the other side.

Example

Solve:
$5x - 2 = 3x + 10$
$5x - 2 - 3x = 10$ ← Subtract 3x from both sides.
$5x - 3x = 10 + 2$ ← Add 2 to both sides.
$2x = 12$
$x = \dfrac{12}{2}$ ← Divide each side by 2.
$x = 6$

Brackets are often included in more complicated equations. Don't be put off though, it's just the same as solving other equations once the brackets have been multiplied out.

Examples

Solve:

(a) $4(2n - 1) = 10$
$8n - 4 = 10$
$8n = 10 + 4$
$8n = 14$
$n = \dfrac{14}{8} = \dfrac{7}{4}$

Multiply the brackets out first.

Solve as before.

(b) $4(2n + 5) = 3(n - 10)$
$8n + 20 = 3n - 30$
$8n + 20 - 3n = -30$
$5n = -50$
$n = -\dfrac{50}{5} = -10$

> Don't forget the negative sign in **(b)**.

(Level 8) Some of the previous equations had solutions involving fractions. Some equations have fractions in them.

> It is easier to remove the fractions first by multiplying each side by the LCM of the denominators of the fractions.

Example

Solve:
$\dfrac{(x - 3)}{2} = \dfrac{(2x + 3)}{3}$

$3(x - 3) = 2(2x + 3)$

$3x - 9 = 4x + 6$

$-9 = 4x - 3x + 6$

$-9 - 6 = x$

$-15 = x \text{ or } x = -15$

Multiply each side by 6.

Expand the brackets.

Subtract $3x$ from both sides.

Subtract 6 from each side.

Using equations to solve problems

When setting up equations, the information you are given will include an unknown quantity. State the letter you decide to use to represent this quantity.

Examples

(a) The lengths of the sides of a triangle are given in the diagram below.
    (i) Write down an expression for the perimeter of the triangle.
        Perimeter $= (x + 2) + (3x - 3) + (2x + 4)$
                 $= 6x + 3$
    (ii) If the perimeter of the triangle is 39cm, form an equation and solve it to find the length of each side. 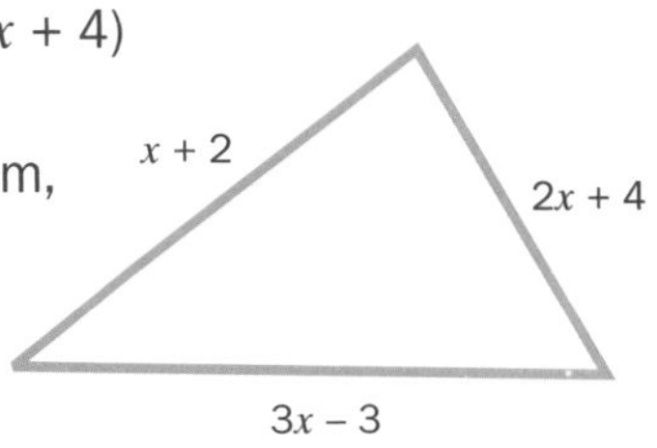
        $6x + 3 = 39$
        $6x = 39 - 3$
        $6x = 36$
         $x = \dfrac{36}{6} = 6$

> The perimeter is found by adding the three lengths.

    The sides are: $x + 2 = 8$cm
                  $2x + 4 = 16$cm
                  $3x - 3 = 15$cm

$x + 2$ $2x + 4$

$3x - 3$

(b) In this triangular arithmagon, what could the numbers x, y and z be? (In an arithmagon, the number in a square is the sum of the numbers in the two circles on either side of it.)

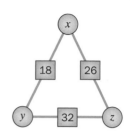

Let x stand for the number in the top circle. Two expressions can be formed for the other two numbers in the circles. Then form an equation to find x.

Since $x + y = 18$	rearranging	$y = 18 - x$
and $x + z = 26$	rearranging	$z = 26 - x$
and $y + z = 32$	this equation becomes	$(18 - x) + (26 - x) = 32$
		$44 - 2x = 32$
		$44 - 32 = 2x$
		$12 = 2x$
So $x = 6$, $y = 12$, $z = 20$.		$x = 6$

Simultaneous linear equations

Two equations both with two unknowns are called **simultaneous linear equations**. They can be solved in several ways. Solving equations simultaneously involves finding values for the letters that will make both equations work.

Elimination method

If the coefficient of one of the letters is the same in both equations then that letter can be eliminated by adding or subtracting the equations.

Example

Solve simultaneously $n + 3p = 25$, $2n + p = 15$.

$n + 3p = 25$	①	Label the equations ① and ②.
$2n + p = 15$	②	As no coefficients match, multiply equation ② by 3.
$6n + 3p = 45$	③	The coefficients of p are now the same in equations ① and ③.
$5n + 0p = 20$		Subtract equation ① from equation ③.
So $5n = 20$		
i.e. $n = 4$		

> A coefficient is a number in front of a letter. For example, 2 is the coefficient of $2n$.

$2n + p = 15$ — Substitute the value of $n = 4$ into equation ① or ②.

so $8 + p = 15$

i.e. $p = 7$

Check in equation ①: $4 + 3 \times 7 = 25$. The solution is $n = 4$, $p = 7$.
(As a further check, substitute $n = 4$, $p = 7$ into the other equation.)

Key Point

To eliminate terms with **opposite** signs, **add** the two equations.
To eliminate terms with **the same** signs, **subtract** the two equations.

Substitution method

Simultaneous equations can also be solved by writing one of the equations in the form '$x = ...$' or '$y = ...$'. This is called **substitution**.

Example

Solve $2x - y = 2$ ①
$3x + 2y = 17$ ②

Rearrange equation ① to give $2x - 2 = y$

Now in the form $y = '...$'

Substitute $2x - 2 = y$ into equation ②.
$3x + 2(2x - 2) = 17$ ← *Work out the value of x from this equation.*
$3x + 4x - 4 = 17$
$7x = 17 + 4$
$7x = 21$
$x = 3$

$y = 2x - 2$ ← *Substitute 3 for x in the first equation.*
$y = 2 \times 3 - 2$
$y = 4$
$x = 3, y = 4$ ← *Remember to check your solution.*

Graphical method

Key Point

The point at which two straight-line graphs **intersect** also gives the **simultaneous solution** of their equations.

Example

Solve the simultaneous equations $y = 2x - 3$, $y - x = 1$ by a graphical method.

Draw the two graphs:

$y = 2x - 3$ if $x = 0$, $y = -3$
                 if $y = 0$, $x = \frac{3}{2}$

You could check on a graphical calculator.

$y - x = 1$ if $x = 0$, $y = 1$
              if $y = 0$, $x = -1$

At the point of intersection $x = 4$ and $y = 5$.

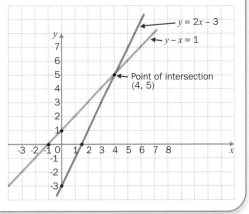

Solving cubic equations by trial and improvement

In trial and improvement, successive approximations are made in order to get closer to the correct value.

Using a spreadsheet is a lot quicker.

Example

The equation $x^3 - 5x = 10$ has a solution between 2 and 3. Find this solution to two decimal places.

Drawing a table may help and then substitute different values of x into $x^3 - 5x$.

x	$x^3 - 5x$	Comment
2.5	3.125	Too small
2.8	7.952	Too small
2.9	9.889	Too small
2.95	10.922 375	Too big
2.94	10.712 184	Too big
2.91	10.092 171	Too big

At this stage the solution is trapped between 2.90 and 2.91
Checking the middle value $x = 2.905$ gives $x^3 - 5x = 9.990\,36...$
which is too small. Because $x = 2.905$ is too small, the solution is
2.91 correct to two decimal places.

2.90	2.905	2.91
(Too small)	(Too small)	(Too big)

Inequalities

Key Point

(Level 7) **Inequalities** are solved in a similar way to equations. Multiplying and dividing by **negative numbers** changes the **direction of the sign**. For example, if $-x \geqslant 5$ then $x \leqslant -5$.

The four inequality symbols are:
- $>$ means 'greater than'
- $\geqslant$ means 'greater than or equal to'
- $<$ means 'less than'
- $\leqslant$ means 'less than or equal to'.

Notice that $x > 3$ and $3 < x$ both mean 'x is greater than 3'.

Examples

Solve the following inequalities.

(a) $4x - 2 < 6$
$$4x < 6 + 2 \quad \longleftarrow \boxed{\text{Add 2 to both sides.}}$$
$$4x < 8$$
$$x < \frac{8}{4} \quad \longleftarrow \boxed{\text{Divide both sides by 4.}}$$
$$x < 2$$

Use ● when the end point is included and ○ when the end point is not included.

The solution of the inequality can be represented on a number line:

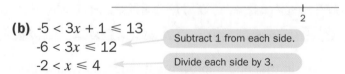

2

(b) $-5 < 3x + 1 \leqslant 13$
$$-6 < 3x \leqslant 12 \quad \longleftarrow \boxed{\text{Subtract 1 from each side.}}$$
$$-2 < x \leqslant 4 \quad \longleftarrow \boxed{\text{Divide each side by 3.}}$$

The integer values that satisfy the above inequality are -1, 0, 1, 2, 3, 4.

Graphs of inequalities

Level 8 The graph of the equation $y = 3$ is a straight line, whereas the graph of the inequality $y < 3$ is a region that has the line $y = 3$ as its **boundary**.

This is how to show the region for given inequalities:
- Draw the boundary lines first.
- For **strict** inequalities > and <, the boundary line is not included and is shown as a dotted line.
- It is often easier with several inequalities to shade out the unwanted regions, so that the solution is shown **unshaded**.

For example, the diagram shows unshaded the region $x > 1$, $x + y \leqslant 4$, $y \geqslant 0$.

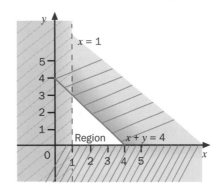

Progress Check

1. Solve the following equations.
   (a) $5x - 2 = 12$
   (b) $4x + 2 = 18$
   (c) $5x + 3 = 2x + 9$
   (d) $6x - 1 = 15 + 2x$
   (e) $3(x + 2) = x + 4$
   (f) $2(x - 1) = 6(2x + 2)$
   (g) $3(n + 1) + 4(n + 2) = 39$

2. **(a)** The perimeter of this rectangle is 74cm. Write down an equation for the perimeter.
   (b) Solve the equation to find the length and width of the rectangle.

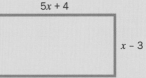

3. The equation $y^3 + y = 40$ has a solution between 3 and 4. Find this solution to 1 d.p. by using a method of trial and improvement. 🖩

4. **Level 7** Solve the following pairs of simultaneous equations.
   (a) $4x + 7y = 10$ **(b)** $3a - 5b = 1$
   $\quad\;\, 2x + 3y = 3$ $\quad\;\, 2a + 3b = 7$

5. **Level 7** Solve the following inequalities.
   (a) $2x - 3 < 9$ **(b)** $5x + 1 \geqslant 21$ **(c)** $1 \leqslant 3x - 2 \leqslant 7$

6. **Level 8** Solve: $\dfrac{3(b + 3)}{4} = \dfrac{(2b + 3)}{2}$

6. 3
5. (a) $x < 6$ (b) $x \geqslant 4$ (c) $1 \leqslant x \leqslant 3$
4. (a) $x = -4.5$, $y = 4$ (b) $a = 2$, $b = 1$
3. 3.3
2. (a) $12x + 2 = 74$ (b) $x = 6$, $l = 34$, $w = 3$
1. (a) $x = 2.8$ (b) $x = 4$ (c) $x = 2$ (d) $x = 4$ (e) $x = -1$ (f) $x = -1.4$ (g) $n = 4$

Assessment questions

Try the following questions.

Level 4 **1.** Isabelle buys some magazines. To work out the cost, she uses the following formula:

> Cost of magazine = cost of one magazine × number bought

The cost of one magazine is £2.45
Isabelle buys four magazines. Find the total cost of the magazines. _____

Level 4 **2.** Richard has n books in his bag. Louise has 5 more books than Richard. Rani has 3 times as many books as Louise. Complete the table showing the number of books each person has.

Person	Number of books
Richard	n
Louise	_____
Rani	_____
Total	_____

Level 5 **3.** In this wall, the expression on each brick is the sum of the two expressions below it. Fill in the missing expressions.

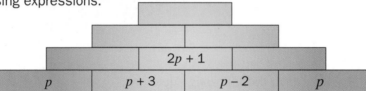

	$2p + 1$	
p	$p + 3$	$p - 2$	p

Level 5 **4.** Each expression in a rectangle is equal to an expression in an oval. For example, $n + n + n = 3n$. Draw a line between pairs of equal expressions.

$n + n + n$	n^3
$2(n - 1)$	$8n + 4$
$5(n + 1) - 2$	$3n$
$n \times n \times n$	$2n - 2$
$5n - 4n$	$5n + 3$
$4(2n + 1)$	n

Level 5 **5.** Complete the missing values in this table.

p	$p + 2$	$2p - 1$	$3p$	$4(p - 2)$
2	_____	_____	_____	_____
_____	_____	9	_____	_____
_____	_____	_____	_____	32

Level 5 **6.** Here are two algebra cards:

$(2y)^2$ $2y^2$

When $y = 4$, $(2y)^2$ is 64.
When $y = 4$, $2y^2$ is not 64.
What is the value of $2y^2$ when $y = 4$? _____

Level 5 **7.** Expand $5(3x - 4)$ _____

Assessment questions

(Level 5) **8.** Work out the value of $(c + d)(c - d)$ when $c = 5.2$ and $d = 3.8$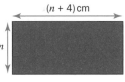

_____

(Level 6) **9.** Solve the following equations:
    (a) $2n + 1 = 11$ _____ **(b)** $5y = 3y + 12$ _____

    (c) $6p + 4 = 3p + 10$ _____ **(d)** $5 - 2y = 3(y + 5)$ _____

    (e) $6(y + 2) = 18$ _____

(Level 6) **10.** Factorise the following expressions:

    (a) $10a + 15$ _____ **(b)** $6p^3 + 3p^2$ _____

(Level 6) **11.** A rectangle has a length of $(2n + 1)$cm and a width of 4cm.
    (a) Write an expression for the perimeter of the rectangle.
        Simplify as much as possible. _____
    (b) The perimeter of the rectangle is 22cm. Write an equation
        involving n and solve it to find the value of n. _____
    (c) How long is the rectangle? _____

(Level 6) **12.** This is what Tom wrote. $\dfrac{1}{a} + \dfrac{2}{b} = \dfrac{3}{a + b}$
    Show that Tom is wrong. _____

(Level 7) **13.** Solve these simultaneous equations:
    (a) $4a + b = 44$ **(b)** $a - 2b = 5$
         $a + b = 20$ _____ $2a + 5b = 100$ _____

(Level 7) **14.** The length of one side of a rectangle is n. An expression for the area
    of the rectangle is $n(n + 4)$. If the area of the rectangle is 50.76cm^2,
    find the value of n by a method of trial and improvement, giving
    the value of n to 1 decimal place. _____

(Level 7) **15.** Solve these inequalities. Mark the solution set on a number line.
    (a) $3n + 5 < 17$ _____ **(b)** $1 \leqslant 5n - 1 < 9$ _____

(Level 8) **16.** Multiply out and simplify:
    (a) $(a + 2)(a - 3)$ _____ **(b)** $(4a + 3)^2$ _____

(Level 8) **17.** This is a formula used in physics: $v^2 = u^2 + 2as$
    Find the value of v when $u = 12$, $a = -3.2$ and $s = 4$, to 1 d.p. _____

(Level 8) **18.** Simplify:
    (a) $p^4 \times p^7$ _____ **(b)** $12p^6 \div 3p^4$ _____

    (c) p^0 _____ **(d)** $p^9 \div p^{11}$ _____

    (e) $(2p^3)^4$ _____

(Level 8) **19.** Factorise the following:
    (a) $x^2 + 9x + 18$ _____ **(b)** $x^2 - 5x + 6$ _____

    (c) $x^2 - 81$ _____ **(d)** $x^2 + 2x - 24$ _____

4 Sequences, functions and graphs

Learning Summary

After studying this section you should be able to:

- generate terms of a sequence and write an expression to describe the nth term of a sequence
- find the next term and the nth term of a quadratic sequence
- draw, interpret and identify graphs of a variety of functions
- construct functions arising from real-life problems

4.1 Sequences and functions

Sequences

A **sequence** is a list of numbers. There is usually a relationship between the numbers. Each value in the list is called a **term**.

There are lots of different number patterns. When finding a missing number in the number pattern, it is sensible to look for the 'term-to-term' rule.

A term-to-term rule tells you the next term by looking at the difference between consecutive terms.

For example:

1, 3, 5, 7, 9... The rule for this pattern is to add 2 each time.
+2 +2 +2 +2 The term-to-term rule here is + 2.

2, 6, 18, 54... The rule for this pattern is to multiply the previous term
×3 ×3 ×3 by 3. The term-to-term rule here is × 3.

1, 1, 2, 3, 5, 8... The rule is to add the two previous numbers
1+1 1+2 2+3 3+5 each time. This sequence is known as the **Fibonacci sequence**.

Some common number patterns you need to recognise are:

- 1, 4, 9, 16, 25...   square numbers
- 1, 8, 27, 64, 125...   cube numbers
- 1, 3, 6, 10, 15...   triangular numbers
- 2, 4, 8, 16, 32...   powers of 2
- 10, 100, 1000, 10 000, 100 000... powers of 10

Finding the nth term of a linear sequence

The nth term is sometimes denoted by **T(n)**, where:

- T(1) = first term
- T(2) = second term
- T(n) = nth term, etc.

For a linear sequence, the nth term takes the form T(n) = $an + b$.

If you plot the term numbers (1, 2, 3, ...) against the terms of a linear sequence, the graph is a straight line.

> **Examples**
>
> **(a)** If T(n) = $3n - 1$, write down the first five terms of the sequence:
> $n = 1$ T(1) = $3 \times 1 - 1 = 2$
> $n = 2$ T(2) = $3 \times 2 - 1 = 5$
> $n = 3$ T(3) = $3 \times 3 - 1 = 8$
> $n = 4$ T(4) = $3 \times 4 - 1 = 11$
> $n = 5$ T(5) = $3 \times 5 - 1 = 14$
> The first five terms are 2, 5, 8, 11, 14.
>
> **(b)** Find the nth term of this sequence: 4, 7, 10, 13, 16, ...
> Look at the difference between the terms. If the difference is the same number this is the value of a or the **multiple**.
> Adjust the rule by adding or subtracting a value, which is b.
>
> | Term | 1 | 2 | 3 | 4 | 5.....n |
> |---|---|---|---|---|---|
> | Sequence | 4 | 7 | 10 | 13 | 16 |
>
> 1st difference   3   3   3   3
>
> The **multiple** is **3**, i.e. $3n$.
> If $n = 1$ then $3 \times 1 = 3$ but we need 4, so we adjust by adding 1.
> nth term **T(n) = $3n + 1$**.
> Check with the second term T(2) = $3 \times 2 + 1 = 7$

Finding the nth term of a quadratic sequence

(Level 7) For a **quadratic sequence**, the first differences are not constant but the second differences are.

The nth term T(n) takes the form T(n) = $an^2 + bn + c$, where b and c may be zero. If you plot the term numbers against the terms of a quadratic sequence, the graph is a parabola.

> **Examples**
>
> **(a)** For the sequence of square numbers find an expression for the nth term.
>
>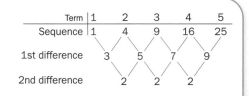
>
> | Term | 1 | 2 | 3 | 4 | 5 |
> |---|---|---|---|---|---|
> | Sequence | 1 | 4 | 9 | 16 | 25 |
>
> 1st difference   3   5   7   9
>
> 2nd difference   2   2   2
>
> Since the second differences are the same, the rule for the nth term is quadratic. In this case, the nth term is n^2.

(b) Find the nth term of this sequence.

Term	1	2	3	4	5
Sequence	3	9	19	33	51
1st difference		6	10	14	18
2nd difference			4	4	4

Since the second differences are the same then the rule for the nth term is quadratic.
The coefficient of n^2 is (second difference) $\div$ 2
i.e. $4 \div 2 = 2$
Adjusting as with linear sequences gives $2n^2 + 1$.

(c) Find the first five terms of the sequence $T(n) = n^2 + 2n - 1$.
$T(1) = 1^2 + 2 \times 1 - 1 = 2$
$T(2) = 2^2 + 2 \times 2 - 1 = 7$
$T(3) = 3^2 + 2 \times 3 - 1 = 14$
$T(4) = 4^2 + 2 \times 4 - 1 = 23$
$T(5) = 5^2 + 2 \times 5 - 1 = 34$

Fraction sequences

(Level 7) When finding the nth term of fraction sequences, it is usually better to look at the numerator and denominator separately.

Examples

Find the nth term of the following fraction sequences:

(a) $\dfrac{1}{2}, \dfrac{2}{3}, \dfrac{3}{4}, \dfrac{4}{5} \ldots$ $T(n) = \dfrac{n}{n+1}$

(b) $\dfrac{1}{2}, \dfrac{1}{4}, \dfrac{1}{6}, \dfrac{1}{8} \ldots$ $T(n) = \dfrac{1}{2n}$

(c) $\dfrac{1}{2}, \dfrac{1}{4}, \dfrac{1}{8}, \dfrac{1}{16} \ldots$ $T(n) = \dfrac{1}{2^n} = 2^{-n}$

Generating sequences from practical examples

The nth term can usually be found by looking at the practical context from which it arose.

For example:

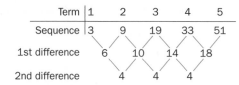

> Using the nth term is particularly useful when doing investigational pieces of work.

Number of squares	1	2	3	4	...
Number of matches	4	7	10	13	...

In the nth arrangement $T(n) = 3n + 1$.
This can be justified by looking at the structure of the shape: each square needs three matches plus an extra one for the first square. For n squares, $3n$ matches are needed plus 1 for the first square.

Function machines and mapping

Function machines are useful when finding a relationship between two **variables**.

For example:

Input (x) ⟶ [x 2] ⟶ [+ 1] ⟶ Output (y)

When numbers are fed into this machine they are first multiplied by 2 and 1 is then added.

If 1 is fed in, 3 comes out $(1 \times 2 + 1 = 3)$
If 2 is fed in, 5 comes out $(2 \times 2 + 1 = 5)$, etc.

This transformation can be illustrated with a **mapping diagram**, like this:

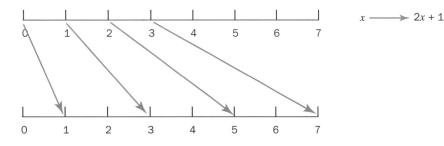

To describe this mapping, write $x \to 2x + 1$.
This is read as 'x **becomes** $2x + 1$'.

(Level 8) Here is another example:

The inverse of $x \to 2x + 1$ is $x \to \dfrac{x - 1}{2}$

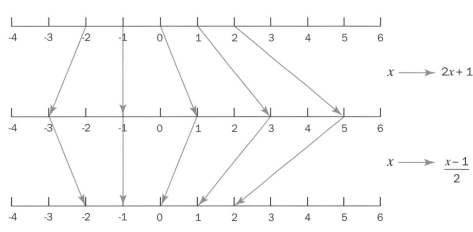

Every function has an **inverse function**, which reverses the direction of the mapping.

Progress Check

1. Continue the following sequences for the next two terms:
   (a) 10, 13, 16, 19, ...   **(b)** $1, \frac{1}{2}, \frac{1}{4}, \frac{1}{8}$, ...   **(c)** 1, -3, 9, -27, ...

2. Find the inverse of these functions:
   (a) $x \to 2x$ **(b)** $x \to 3x - 1$ **(c)** $x \to 3(x - 4)$ **(d)** $x \to \frac{x+2}{5}$

3. True or false? The nth term of $\frac{1}{2}, \frac{1}{4}, \frac{1}{6}, \frac{1}{8}$, ... is $\frac{1}{2n}$.

4. (Level 7) Write down the nth term, $T(n)$, of these sequences:
   (a) 5, 7, 9, 11, ...   **(b)** 7, 10, 13, 16, ...   **(c)** 2, 8, 18, 32, ...

5. (Level 7) Write down the first four terms of these sequences:
   (a) $T(n) = n^2 + 1$ **(b)** $T(n) = 10 - 2n$ **(c)** $T(n) = n^2 + 4n - 6$

5. (a) 2, 5, 10, 17 (b) 8, 6, 4, 2 (c) -1, 6, 15, 26
4. (a) $T(n) = 2n + 3$ (b) $T(n) = 3n + 4$ (c) $T(n) = 2n^2$
3. True
2. (a) $x \to \frac{x}{2}$ (b) $x \to \frac{x+1}{3}$ (c) $x \to \frac{x}{3} + 4$ (d) $x \to 5x - 2$
1. (a) 22, 25 (b) $\frac{1}{16}, \frac{1}{32}$ (c) 81, -243

4.2 Graphs of functions

Coordinates

Coordinates are used to locate the **position** of a point. When reading coordinates read across first, then up or down.

Coordinates are always written in **brackets** and with a **comma** in between, e.g. (2, 4). The **horizontal axis** is the x-axis. The **vertical axis** is the y-axis.

For example:
A has coordinates (2, 4).
B has coordinates (-1, 3).
C has coordinates (-2, -3).
D has coordinates (3, -1).

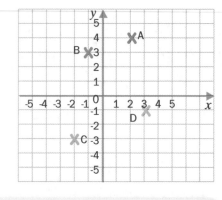

Straight-line graphs

Graphs of the form $x = b$ and $y = a$

Key Point

$y = a$ is a **horizontal line**, with every y-coordinate equal to a.
$x = b$ is a **vertical line**, with every x-coordinate equal to b.

Examples

(a) Draw the line $y = 3$.
(b) Draw the line $x = 2$.

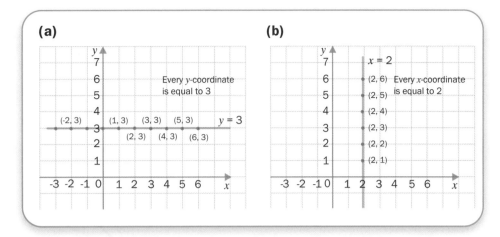

Coordinates are used to draw graphs. Before a graph can be drawn the coordinates have to be worked out.

To work out the coordinates for the graph, you can do either of the following:
- Draw up a table as shown in the examples.
- Use a function machine and mapping diagrams.

Graphs of the form $y = mx + c$

Graphs of the form $y = mx + c$ are straight-line (linear) graphs.

> To draw a straight-line graph you need at least three sets of coordinates.

Example

Draw the graph of $y = 2x + 1$.

Choose some values of x, e.g. -2, 0, 2. Replace x in the function with the given values.

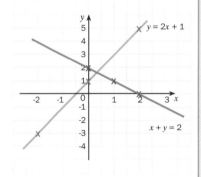

x	$\rightarrow$	$2x + 1$	Coordinates
-2	$\rightarrow$	$(2 \times \text{-}2 + 1) = \text{-}3$	(-2, -3)
0	$\rightarrow$	$(2 \times 0 + 1) = 1$	(0, 1)
2	$\rightarrow$	$(2 \times 2 + 1) = 5$	(2, 5)

Alternatively, a table of values can be used:

x	-2	0	2
y	-3	1	5

Plot the coordinates and join up the points with a straight line. Label the graph.

For the graph $x + y = 2$, choose some values of x and work out the corresponding values of y:
If $x = 0$, $y = 2$; if $x = 1$, $y = 1$; if $x = 2$, $y = 0$

Linear functions can be rearranged to give y in terms of x and the coordinates can be worked out as normal.

For example, if drawing the graphs of:
- $y - 2x + 2 = 0$ rearrange to give $y = 2x - 2$.
- $2y + 3x = 6$ rearrange to give $2y = 6 - 3x$, i.e. $y = 3 - \frac{3}{2}x$.
- $x + y = 2$ rearrange to give $y = 2 - x$ or draw directly $x + y = 2$ (see above).

Key Point

The general equation of a straight-line graph is $y = mx + c$.

m is the **gradient** (steepness) of the line:

- As m **increases**, the line gets **steeper**.
- If m is **positive**, the line **slopes forwards**.
- If m is **negative**, the line **slopes backwards**.

For example:

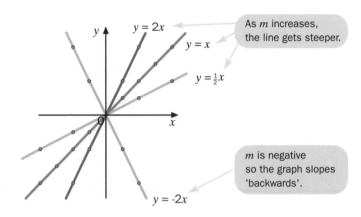

As m increases, the line gets steeper.

m is negative so the graph slopes 'backwards'.

Parallel lines have the same gradient.

c is the **intercept on the y-axis**, that is where the graph cuts the y-axis.

For example:

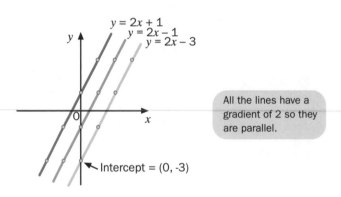

All the lines have a gradient of 2 so they are parallel.

Intercept = (0, -3)

Finding the gradient of a straight line

Key Point

To find the gradient of a straight line, choose any two points on the line.

$$\text{Gradient} = \frac{\text{change in } y}{\text{change in } x}$$

For example:

Choose two points on the line. Find the change in y (height) and the change in x (base).

It is important to remember not just to count the squares as the scales may be different.

$$\text{Gradient} = \frac{\text{change in } y}{\text{change in } x} \text{ or } \frac{\text{height}}{\text{base}} = \frac{4}{3} = 1\frac{1}{3}$$

Decide if the gradient is positive or negative.

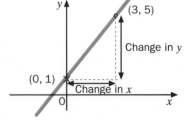

For example **(c)** rearrange into $y = 2x - 5$.

Example

Write down the gradient and intercept for each of these straight-line graphs:

(a) $y = 4x - 3$ **(b)** $y = 6 - 2x$ **(c)** $2y + 10 = 4x$

     Gradient = 4   Gradient = -2   Gradient = 2

     Intercept = (0, -3)   Intercept = (0, 6)   Intercept = (0, -5)

Graphs that are not straight lines

Quadratic graphs

(Level 8) Quadratic graphs are graphs of the form $y = ax^2 + bx + c$ where $a \neq 0$. These graphs are curved.

If the number in front of x^2 is positive, the curve looks like this:

If the number in front of x^2 is negative, the curve looks like this:

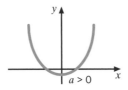

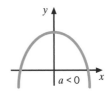

Example

Draw the graph of $y = x^2 - x - 6$ using values of x from -2 to 3. Use the graph to find the value of x when $y = -3$.

Make a table of values:

x	-2	-1	0	1	2	3	0.5
y	0	-4	-6	-6	-4	0	-6.25

$x = 0.5$ is an extra point used to work out the minimum value.

Replace x in the equation with each value, i.e. when $x = -2$,

$y = (-2)^2 - (-2) - 6$

   $= 0$

You can explore different functions on a graphical calculator.

The table represents the coordinates of the graph, which can now be plotted. Join the points with a smooth curve and label the graph.

If you are asked to draw the graph of $y = 2x^2$, remember that this means $y = 2 \times (x^2)$, i.e. square x first and then multiply by 2.

The **minimum** value is when $x = 0.5$, $y = -6.25$.

The **line of symmetry** is at $x = 0.5$.

The curve cuts the y-axis at (0, -6), i.e. (0, c).

To find the value of x when $y = -3$, read across from $y = -3$ to the graph then read up to the x-axis.

$x = 2.3$ and $x = -1.3$. These are the approximate solutions of the equation $x^2 - x - 6 = -3$.

Cubic graphs

(Level 8) When drawing the graph of $y = x^3$, it is important to remember that $x^3 = x \times x \times x$.

> Notice the shape of the graph.

Example

Draw the graph of $y = x^3$.
Work out the y-coordinate for each point.
Replace x in the equation with each value.

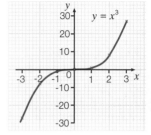

x	-3	-2	-1	0	1	2	3
y	-27	-8	-1	0	1	8	27

Plot the x and y-coordinates from the table above.

Reciprocal graphs

(Level 8) The graph of the equation $y = \dfrac{a}{x}$ takes one of two forms, depending on the value of a.

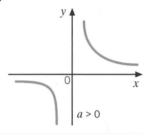

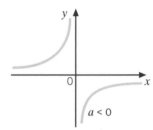

> **Progress Check**

1. The graph of $y = x - 1$ is drawn on the grid opposite. Draw the following graphs on the same axes.
   (a) $y = 2x$ **(b)** $y = 4x$
   (c) What do you notice about the graphs $y = 2x$ and $y = 4x$?
   (d) Without working out any coordinates, draw the graph of $y = x - 2$.

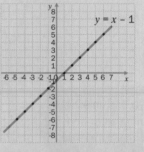

2. (Level 7) Write down the gradient and intercept of each of these straight-line graphs. **(a)** $y = 4x - 1$ **(b)** $y = 3 - 2x$ **(c)** $2y = 4x + 8$.

3. (Level 7) True or false? The gradient of the line $2y = 4x + 6$ is 4.

4. (Level 8) Match each of the three graphs below with one of the following equations:
   - $y = 2x - 5$
   - $y = x^2 + 3$
   - $y = 3 - x^2$
   - $y = 5 - x$
   - $y = x^3$

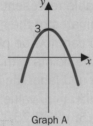

Graph A   Graph B   Graph C

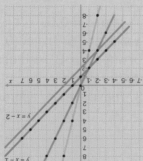

Graph C: $y = x^3$
Graph B: $y = 5 - x$
4. Graph A: $y = 3 - x^2$
3. False
2. (a) Gradient 4 Intercept (0, -1)
(b) Gradient -2 Intercept (0, 3)
(c) Gradient 2 Intercept (0, 4)
(d) See grid opposite.
They both pass through the origin.
(c) $y = 4x$ is steeper than $y = 2x$.
1. (a)–(b) See grid opposite.

4.3 Interpreting graphical information

It is important that you can interpret graphical information from a variety of situations.

Using linear graphs

Linear graphs are often used to show relationships.

For example:
Neville has a window cleaning round. He charges £5 for the use of his materials and £4 per hour after that. This information can be put into a table.

> The equation of this graph is $c = 4h + 5$. The gradient is 4 (i.e. the charge per hour) and the intercept is (0, 5), i.e. the standing charge for his materials.

No. of hrs	0	1	2	3	4	5
Charge (£)	5	9	13	17	21	25

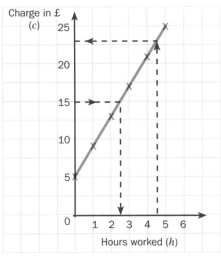

The graph of this information shows that there is a linear relationship.

The graph can be used to find, for example, how long Neville works if he charges £15 ($2\frac{1}{2}$ hours) and what he charges if he works $4\frac{1}{2}$ hours (£23).

Conversion graphs

Conversion graphs are used to change one unit of measurement into another unit; for example, litres to pints, kilometres to miles, pounds to dollars, etc.

For example:
£1 = $1.50

To change dollars to £, read across to the line then read down; for example, $4 = £2.67 (approx.)

To change £ to dollars, read up to the line then read across; for example, £4.50 is $6.80 (approx.)

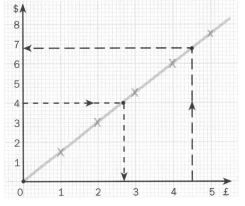

Distance-time graphs

Key Point

Distance-time graphs are often known as **travel graphs**.
Distance is on the **vertical axis**; **time** is on the **horizontal axis**.
The speed of an object can be found on a distance-time graph by using:

$$\text{Speed} = \frac{\text{distance}}{\text{time}}$$

Example

The travel graph shows the car journeys of two people.

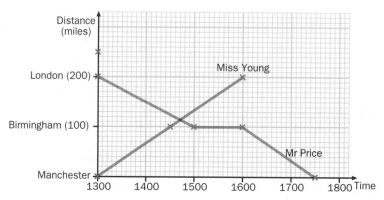

From the travel graph find the following:

(a) The speed at which Miss Young is travelling.

$$\text{Speed} = \frac{\text{distance}}{\text{time}} = \frac{200}{3} = 66.7\text{mph (1 d.p.)}$$

(b) The length of time Mr Price had a break.
Mr Price is stationary between 1500 and 1600, i.e. 1 hour.

(c) The speed of Mr Price from Birmingham to Manchester.

$$\text{Speed} = \frac{\text{distance}}{\text{time}} = \frac{100}{1.5} = 66.7\text{mph (1 d.p.)}$$

(d) The time at which Miss Young and Mr Price pass each other.
Since each small square is 6 minutes, they pass at 1442.

(e) The speed of Mr Price from London to Birmingham.

$$\text{Speed} = \frac{\text{distance}}{\text{time}} = \frac{100}{2} = 50\text{mph}$$

The above example highlights the following key points.

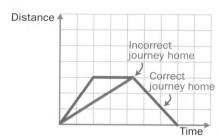

The steeper the graph, the greater
the speed. Object A is **travelling
faster** than object B, which in turn
is travelling faster than object C.

The green line shows an
incorrect journey time because
you cannot **go back** in time.

Matching graphs to real-life situations

Example

Level 8 These containers are being filled with water at a rate of 150ml per second. The graphs show how the depth of the water changes with time. Match the containers with the correct graphs.

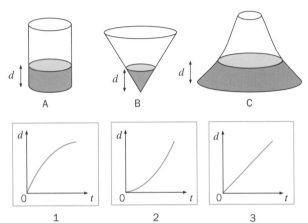

Container A is graph 3 since the depth of the water changes uniformly with time.

Container B is graph 1 since the depth will rise quickly in the narrow part of the cone and then begin to slow down.

Container C is graph 2 because the depth will increase slowly at the wider part of the container and then increase more quickly at the narrow part.

Progress Check

1. The distance-time graph shows Mrs Roberts' car journey.
   (a) At what speed did she travel for the first 2 hours?
   (b) What is happening at A?
   (c) At what speed is her return journey?

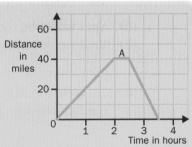

2. The graph shows the charges made by a van-hire firm.
   (a) What do you think point A represents?
   (b) By using the gradient of the line, work out how much was charged per day for the hire of the van.
   (c) Write down a formula that connects the cost (C) of the van hire and the number of days (d).

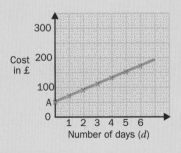

1. (a) 20mph (b) Car is stationary (c) 40mph
2. (a) Point A represents the initial £50 charge for hiring the van.
(b) Gradient = 20. Hence £20 was charged per day.
(c) $C = 20d + 50$

Assessment questions

Try the following questions.

Level 4 **1.** Write down the next two numbers in each sequence:
  (a) 10, 13, 16, 19, _22_, _25_
  (b) 2, 4, 8, 16, _32_, _64_
  (c) 128, 64, 32, 16, _8_, _4_

Level 4 **2.** Fill in the missing numbers in this function machine.

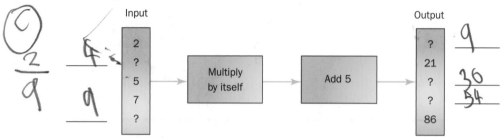

$\frac{2}{9}$ $\frac{4}{9}$ $\frac{9}{9}$

Input			Output
2	Multiply by itself	Add 5	? → 9
?			21
5			? → 36
7			? → 54
?			86

Level 5 **3.** Here is a pattern made up of regular hexagons with sides 1cm.
The table shows the pattern number (*n*) and the perimeter of each shape.

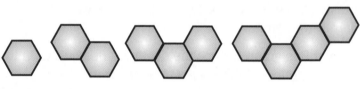

(a) Complete the table.

Pattern number (*n*)	1	2	3	4	5	6
Perimeter (cm)	6	10	14	18	22	26

(b) What would be the perimeter for the *n*th pattern? ___4n + 2___
(c) What would be the perimeter for pattern number 50? ___202___ cm

Level 5 **4.** The grid shows six points labelled A, B, C, D, E, F.
  (a) Complete the table to show which points have coordinates that match the rules below.
    The first line has been done for you.

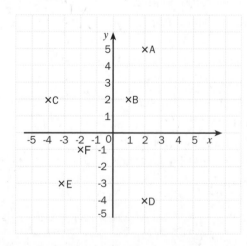

Rule	A	B	C	D	E	F
x = 2	✓	✗	✗	✓	✗	✗
y = 2	✗	✓	✓	✗	✗	✗
y = x + 1	✗	✓	✓	✗	✗	✓

Assessment questions

(b) This grid shows eight different points. One rule matches the coordinates of each of the eight points.

What is the rule that connects x and y? _~~$y = x$~~_ $x + y = 7$

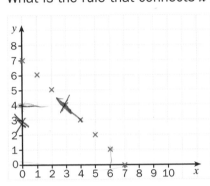

Level 6 **5.** You can write the equation $y = x + 3$ in different ways. Which of these are correct?

    (a) **A** $y - x = 3$ **B** $y + x = 3$ **C** $x = y + 3$
         D $y = 3 + x$ **E** $y - 3 = x$ a, d + e

    (b) The equation of line PQ is $y = x + 3$. Write the equation that describes RS. $y = x - 2$

    (c) On the grid draw the line $y = 2x + 2$.

    (d) What is the gradient of $y = 2x + 2$? _____

    (e) What do you notice about the points where the three lines intercept the y-axis?

_____

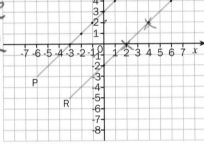

Level 7 **6.** Write down the nth term of each sequence.

    (a) 5, 7, 9, 11, 13, ...   15 17 19 21 23 $T(n) = 2n + 3$ ✓
    (b) 1, 4, 9, 16, 25, ...   36 49 $T(n) = n^2$
    (c) 6, 11, 16, 21, 26, ... $T(n) = 5n + 1$ ✓
    (d) $\frac{1}{4}, \frac{1}{6}, \frac{1}{8}, \frac{1}{10}$, ...   12 14 16 18 20 22 24 $T(n) = \frac{1}{2n + 2}$ ✓

Level 7 **7.** The distance-time graph shows Sinita's journey to work. A shop is 6km from her home.

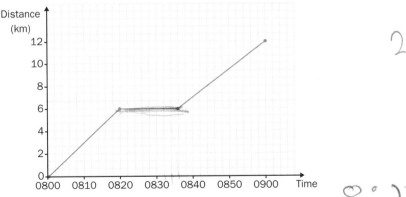

20

    (a) At what time does Sinita stop at the shop? _8:20_
    (b) How long is Sinita at the shop? _16 mins_
    (c) At what speed (km/h) does Sinita travel to the shop? _18_
    (d) At what speed (km/h) does Sinita travel from the shop to work? _15_

Assessment questions

Level 7 **8.** William and Marek are doing an investigation into square numbers. Here are their workings:

William

$3^2 = 3 + 3 \times 2$
$4^2 = 4 + 4 \times 3$
$5^2 = 5 + 5 \times 4$
$6^2 = 6 + 6 \times 5$

Marek

$3^2 = 2 \times 3 + 2 \times 1 + 1$
$4^2 = 2 \times 4 + 3 \times 2 + 2$
$5^2 = 2 \times 5 + 4 \times 3 + 3$
$6^2 = 2 \times 6 + 5 \times 4 + 4$

(a) Write down an expression for n^2 using William's pattern. $n^2 = n + n \times (n-1)$ ✓

(b) Write down Marek's expression for n^2. $n^2 = 2 \times n + (n-1) \times (n-2) + n - 2$ ✓

Level 8 (c) Show that Marek's expression simplifies to n^2. *C*

Level 7 **9.** Here are six different equations, labelled A to F:

$\boxed{A \mid y = 5x + 2}$ $\boxed{B \mid y = 3x - 2}$ $\boxed{C \mid y = 3}$ $\boxed{D \mid x + y = 10}$ $\boxed{E \mid x = -5}$ $\boxed{F \mid y = 2x^2}$

Think about the graphs of these equations.

(a) Which graph passes through the point (0, 0)? *F*

(b) Which graph is parallel to the x-axis? *C*

(c) Which graph is not a straight line? *F*

(d) Which graph passes through the point (0, 10)? *D*

(e) Which graph passes through the point (2, 4)? *B* ✓

Level 8 **10.** Water is poured into these containers at a constant rate.
Match each container to the correct graph.

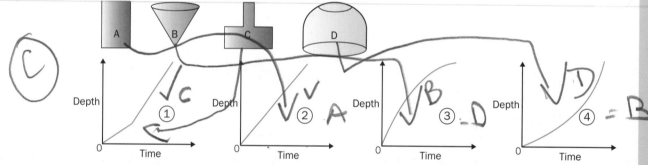

C

Depth ① *C* Depth ② *A* Depth ③ *D* Depth ④ *B*

Time   Time   Time   Time

Level 8 **11.** The diagram opposite shows a sketch of the curve $y = 9 - x^2$.
What are the coordinates of the points A, B and C?

A: (0,9)   B = (3,0)   C = (-3,0)

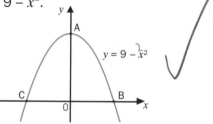

$y = 9 - x^2$ ✓

Level 8 **12.** Here are six different equations, labelled A to F:

A $y = 2 - 5x$ **B** $y = x^2 - 4$ **C** $y = x^3$ **D** $y = 5x - 2$ **E** $y = \frac{2}{x}$ **F** $y = 16 - x^2$

Match each graph to the correct label. (Two labels will not be used.)

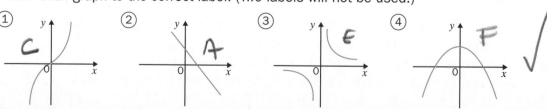

① *C*   ② *A*   ③ *E*   ④ *F* ✓

Geometry and measures

Geometry: lines, angles and shapes		Studied	Revised	Assessment questions
5.1	**Two and three-dimensional shapes**			
	– Two-dimensional shapes – Three-dimensional solids – Plans and elevations – Coordinates in three dimensions – Symmetry – Congruent shapes			
5.2	**Angles, bearings and scale drawings**			
	– Angles and the protractor – Reading angles – Angle facts – Angles in parallel lines – Angles in a polygon – Tessellations – Compass directions and bearings – Scale drawings and bearings – Maps and diagrams			
5.3	**Pythagoras' theorem**			
	– Calculating the length of a line segment – Solving problems			
5.4	**Trigonometry in right-angled triangles**			
	– Trigonometric ratios – Solving problems using trigonometry			

Transformations, constructions and loci		Studied	Revised	Assessment questions
6.1	**Transformations and similarity**			
	– Reflections and translations – Rotations – Enlargements – Combining transformations – Similar figures			
6.2	**Constructions and loci**			
	– Locus			

Measures and measurement		Studied	Revised	Assessment questions
7.1	**Units of measurement**			
	– Estimating – Metric units – Imperial units – Choosing the correct units of measurement – Time measurement – Compound measures			
7.2	**Area and perimeter of 2-D shapes**			
	– Estimating areas of 2-D shapes – Areas of quadrilaterals and triangles – Circumference and area of a circle – Areas of enlarged shapes – Changing area units			
7.3	**Volume of 3-D solids**			
	– Calculating volume and surface area – Volumes of enlarged solids – Converting volume units – Dimensions			

5 Geometry: lines, angles and shapes

Learning Summary

After studying this section you should be able to:

- use a wide range of properties of two and three-dimensional shapes
- classify quadrilaterals by their geometric properties
- understand and use congruence
- use angle properties, bearings and scale drawings
- use and apply Pythagoras' theorem when solving problems in 2-D
- use and apply trigonometry in right-angled triangles when solving problems

5.1 Two and three-dimensional shapes

A straight line is **one-dimensional**. It has only length. A **line segment** is of **finite** length. For example, the line segment PQ has end points P and Q.

P   Q

Two lines are **parallel** if they are in the same direction. They are always **equidistant** (the same distance apart). For example:

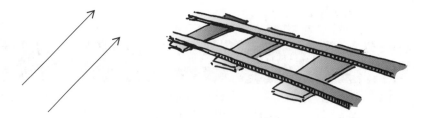

Two lines are **perpendicular** if they are at **right angles** to each other. For example:

> Perpendicular lines meet at 90°.

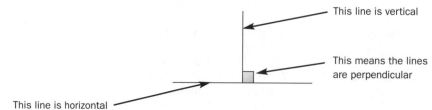

This line is vertical

This means the lines are perpendicular

This line is horizontal

Two-dimensional shapes

Key Point

Two-dimensional (2-D) shapes have area. All points on 2-D shapes are in the same plane. 2-D shapes are often seen in Islamic art.

Below are the 2-D shapes you need to recognise along with some of their important properties.

Triangles

Triangles have **three sides**. There are several types of triangle:

Right-angled Has a 90° angle.	Equilateral Three sides equal. Three angles equal.
Isosceles Two sides equal. Base angles equal.	Scalene All the sides and angles are different.

Quadrilaterals

Quadrilaterals have **four sides**. There are several types of quadrilateral:

Bisect means to cut in half.

Square • Four lines of symmetry • Rotational symmetry of order 4 • All angles are 90° • All sides equal • Two pairs of parallel sides • The diagonals are equal and bisect each other at right angles	Rectangle • Two lines of symmetry • Rotational symmetry of order 2 • All angles are 90° • Opposite sides equal • Two pairs of parallel sides • The diagonals bisect each other
Parallelogram • No lines of symmetry • Rotational symmetry of order 2 • Opposite sides are equal and parallel • Opposite angles are equal	Rhombus • Two lines of symmetry • Rotational symmetry of order 2 • All sides are equal • Opposite sides are parallel • Opposite angles are equal • The diagonals bisect each other at right angles and also bisect the corner angles
Kite • One line of symmetry • No rotational symmetry • Diagonals do not bisect each other • Two pairs of adjacent sides are equal • Diagonals cross at right angles	Trapezium • Has one pair of parallel sides • No lines of symmetry • No rotational symmetry • An isosceles trapezium has one line of symmetry

Polygons

Polygons are 2-D shapes with straight sides. **Regular polygons** are shapes with all sides and angles equal.

Number of sides	Name of polygon
3	Triangle
4	Quadrilateral
5	Pentagon
6	Hexagon
7	Heptagon
8	Octagon
9	Nonagon
10	Decagon

Regular pentagon
- Five equal sides
- Rotational symmetry of order 5
- Five lines of symmetry

Regular hexagon
- Six equal sides
- Rotational symmetry of order 6
- Six lines of symmetry

Regular octagon
- Eight equal sides
- Rotational symmetry of order 8
- Eight lines of symmetry

The circle

> Remember that the diameter is twice the length of the radius.

The **circumference** is the distance around the outside edge of a circle. The **diameter** is twice the **radius**.

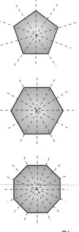

A **chord** is a line that joins two points on the circumference. A chord does not go through the centre.
An **arc** is part of the circumference.

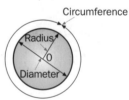

> It is important that you learn these key facts about circles.

A **tangent** touches the circle at one point only.
The radius and tangent at a point make an **angle of 90°**.

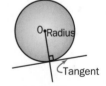

The **perpendicular bisector** of a chord passes through the centre of a circle.

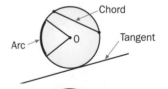

The angle in a semicircle is always a **right angle**.

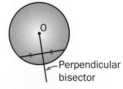

Three-dimensional solids

Below are some of the 3-D solids you should know.

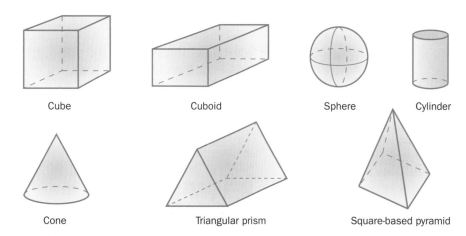

| Cube | Cuboid | Sphere | Cylinder |

| Cone | Triangular prism | Square-based pyramid |

A **prism** is a solid which can be cut into slices that are all the same shape.

A **face** is a flat surface of a solid.

An **edge** is where two faces meet.

Vertex is another word for corner. The plural is **vertices**.

The **net** of a 3-D solid is a 2-D (flat) shape that can be folded to make the 3-D solid.

For example:

- A cuboid has 6 faces, 8 vertices and 12 edges.

Face

Vertex

Edge

The net of the cuboid would look like this:

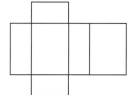

- You can represent 3-D shapes on **isometric paper**. On this paper you can draw lengths in three perpendicular directions on the same scale. The faces do not appear in their true shape.

- A 'T'-shaped prism can be shown clearly on isometric paper.

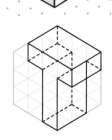

Plans and elevations

Key Point

A **plan** is what can be seen if a 3-D solid is looked down on from above. An **elevation** is seen if the 3-D solid is looked at from the side or front.

Architects often use plans to show the design of new properties.

Example

Draw a sketch of the plan and the elevations from A and B of this solid.

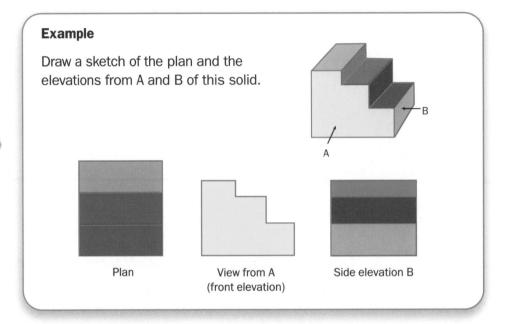

Plan

View from A
(front elevation)

Side elevation B

Coordinates in three dimensions

(Level 7) This involves the extension of the normal x-y coordinates into a **third direction**, known as z. All positions have three coordinates (x, y, z).

For example, in this cuboid, the vertices have the following coordinates:

A (3, 0, 0)
B (3, 2, 0)
C (0, 2, 0)
D (0, 2, 1)
E (0, 0, 1)
F (3, 0, 1)
G (3, 2, 1)
O (0, 0, 0)

Remember to read in the order (x, y, z).

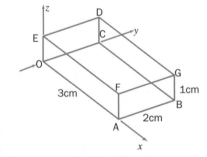

Symmetry

There are three different types of symmetry.

Reflective symmetry

Reflective symmetry is when both sides of a shape are the same on each side of a **mirror line**. The mirror line is known as a **line** or **axis of symmetry**.

For example:

| 1 line of symmetry | 1 line of symmetry | 3 lines of symmetry | No line of symmetry |

Example

Half a reflected shape is shown here. The dashed line is the line of symmetry. Copy and complete this shape.

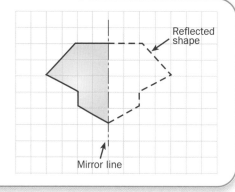

Reflected shape

Mirror line

Rotational symmetry

A 2-D shape has **rotational symmetry** if, when it is turned, it looks exactly the same. The **order** of rotational symmetry is the number of times the shape can be turned and still look the same.

For example:

> For the kite, there is one position. It is said to have **rotational symmetry of order 1** or **no rotational symmetry**.

 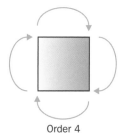 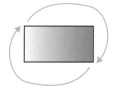

| Order 1 (no rotational symmetry) | Order 4 | Order 2 |

Plane symmetry

Key Point

Plane symmetry only exists in 3-D solids. A 3-D solid has a **plane of symmetry** if the plane divides the shape into two halves, and one half is the exact **mirror image** of the other. 3-D solids can have more than one plane of symmetry.

For example:

> When drawing in a plane of symmetry, you must show its edges.

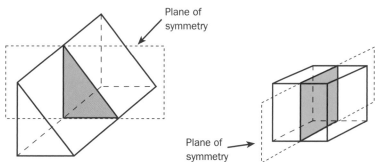

Plane of symmetry

Plane of symmetry

Congruent shapes

Key Point

(Level 8) Shapes are **congruent** if they are exactly the same size and shape, i.e. identical. Two shapes are congruent even if they are mirror images of each other.

Triangles are congruent if one of the following sets of conditions is true: (S stands for side, A for angle, R for right angle, H for hypotenuse.)

SSS – The three sides of one triangle are the same as the three sides of the other triangle.

SAS – Two sides and the angle between them in one triangle are equal to two sides and the angle between them in the other triangle.

RHS – Each triangle contains a right angle. Both hypotenuses and another pair of sides are equal.

AAS – Two angles and a side in one triangle are equal to two angles and the corresponding side in the other.

Progress Check

1. Draw an accurate net of this 3-D shape.

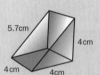

2. True or false? A rectangle has rotational symmetry of order 2.
3. Draw a plane of symmetry on this solid.

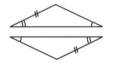

4. Which is correct? A five-sided polygon is called a:
   A pentagon **B** quadrilateral **C** hexagon **D** octagon **E** heptagon.
5. (Level 8) Are these two triangles congruent? Explain why.

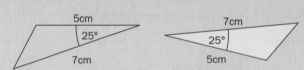

4. **A** pentagon   5. Yes, congruent because SAS, i.e. two sides and the included angle are equal.

3. (or a vertical plane at right angles to this one)   2. True   1.

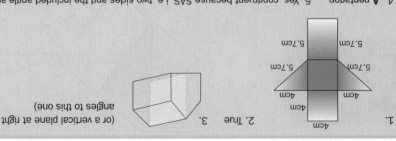

5.2 Angles, bearings and scale drawings

Angles and the protractor

An angle is the amount of turning or rotation. Angles are measured in **degrees**. A circle is divided into 360 parts. Each part is called a degree and is represented by a small circle, °.

Key Point

An **acute angle** is between 0° and 90°.

An **obtuse angle** is between 90° and 180°.

A **reflex angle** is between 180° and 360°.

A **right angle** is 90°.

A protractor is used to measure the size of an angle:
- Make sure you put 0° at the start position, and that you read from the correct scale.
- For this angle, measure on the outer scale since you must start at 0°.

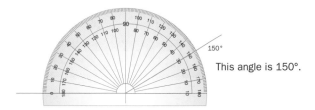

This angle is 150°.

Reading angles

When asked to find angle XYZ or ∠XYZ or XŶZ, find the middle letter angle, i.e. at Y:

XŶZ = 30°

Angle facts

There are some angle facts that you need to learn:
- Angles on a **straight line** add up to **180°**.

- Angles in a **triangle** add up to **180°**.

- **Vertically opposite** angles are **equal**.

- Angles at a **point** add up to **360°**.

- Angles in a **quadrilateral** add up to **360°**.

- An **exterior** angle of a triangle equals the **sum of the two opposite interior angles**. $c = a + b$.

Examples

Find the angles labelled by letters:

(a) $a + 135° = 180°$
$a = 180° - 135°$
$a = 45°$

(b) $p + 90° + 120° = 360°$
$p + 210° = 360°$
$p = 360° - 210°$
$p = 150°$

> In an isosceles triangle, the base angles are equal.

(c) $a + a + 80° = 180$
$2a + 80° = 180°$
$2a = 180° - 80°$
$2a = 100°$
$a = 50°$

(d) $a + 110° = 180°$
$a = 70°$
$40° + b = 110°$
$b = 110° - 40°$
$b = 70°$

Angles in parallel lines

> **Key Point**

Alternate (z) angles are **equal**.	Corresponding angles are **equal**.	Interior angles add up to **180°**. $c + d = 180°$

> Interior angles are also known as **supplementary angles**.

For example:

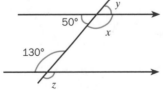

$x = 130°$ (alternate)
$y = 50°$ (vertically opposite)
$z = 130°$ (vertically opposite)

$a = 120°$ (angles on a straight line)
$b = 60°$ (vertically opposite)
$c = 60°$ (alternate)
$d = 60°$ (vertically opposite to c).

Angles in a polygon

There are two types of angle in a polygon: **interior** (inside) and **exterior** (outside).

For any polygon with n sides:
- sum of exterior angles = 360°

For a regular polygon with n sides:
- size of exterior angle = $\dfrac{360°}{n}$
- **interior angle + exterior angle = 180°**
- **sum of interior angles = $(n - 2) \times 180°$**

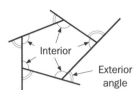

Interior

Exterior angle

Examples

(a) Calculate the interior and exterior angle of a regular hexagon.

A hexagon has six sides.

Exterior angle = $\dfrac{360°}{6}$ = 60°

Interior angle = 180° − 60°
$\qquad\qquad$ = 120°

(b) Find the sum of the interior angles of a regular pentagon.

A pentagon has five sides.
Sum of interior angles = $(n - 2) \times 180°$
$\qquad\qquad\qquad\qquad$ = $(5 - 2) \times 180°$
$\qquad\qquad\qquad\qquad$ = $3 \times 180°$
$\qquad\qquad\qquad\qquad$ = 540°

Tessellations

A **tessellation** is a pattern of 2-D shapes that fit together without leaving any gaps. Tessellations are seen throughout the history of art, from ancient to modern art. They frequently appear in the art of M.C. Escher.

Here are some examples of tessellations:

For shapes to tessellate, the angles at each point must add up to 360°.

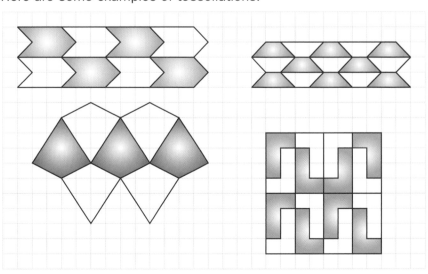

Compass directions and bearings

The diagram shows the points of the compass. Directions can also be given as bearings. Bearings are used on aeroplanes and ships to make sure they are travelling in the right direction and to avoid collisions.

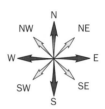

Key Point

Bearings give directions in degrees. They are always measured from the **North** in a **clockwise** direction.

A bearing must have **three figures**. The word '**from**' indicates the position of the north line from which the angle is measured.

For example:

Since we are finding the bearing of P from Q, the north line is placed at Q. The bearing is measured in a clockwise direction from this north line.

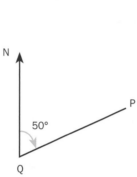

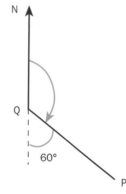

Bearing of P from Q	Bearing of P from Q	Bearing of P from Q
= 050°	= 180° – 60°	= 360° – 70°
	= 120°	= 290°

When finding a **back bearing**, that is the bearing of Q from P in the diagrams above:

- Draw a north line at P.
- The two north lines are parallel lines, so the angle properties of parallel lines are used.

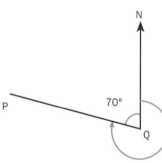

For example:
- Put the north line at P.
  Measure in a clockwise direction from P.
  Bearing of Q from P is 50° + 180° = 230°.

- Put the north line at P.
  Measure in a clockwise direction from P.
  Bearing of Q from P is 360° – 60° = 300°.

Scale drawings and bearings

Scale drawings are very useful for finding lengths that cannot be measured directly.

When drawing scale diagrams, the lengths need to be accurate to 2mm and the angles to 2°.

Example

A ship sails from a harbour for 15km on a bearing of 040°, and then continues due east for 20km. Make a scale drawing of this journey using a scale of 1cm to 5km. How far will the ship have to sail to get back to the harbour by the shortest route? What will the bearing be?

Shortest route = 6.4 × 5km
= 32km

Bearing = 70° + 180°
= 250°

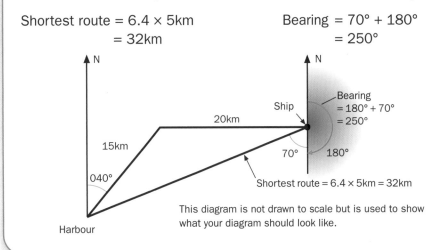

This diagram is not drawn to scale but is used to show what your diagram should look like.

Maps and diagrams

Scales are often used on maps and diagrams. They are usually written as **ratios**.

Examples

(a) The scale on a road map is 1 : 25 000. Manchester and Rochdale are 60cm apart on the map. Work out the real distance between them in km.

On a scale of 1 : 25 000, 1cm on the map represents 25 000cm on the ground.

60cm represents 60 × 25 000 = 1 500 000cm.

Divide by 100 to change cm to m.
1 500 000 ÷ 100 = 15 000m
Divide by 1000 to change m to km.
15 000 ÷ 1000 = 15km.
Distance between Manchester and Rochdale is 15km.

(b) A house plan has a scale of 1 : 30. If the width of the house on the plan is 64cm, what width is the real house?

1cm represents 30cm.
64cm represents 64 × 30 = 1920cm.
1920 ÷ 100 = 19.2m.
The width of the house is 19.2m.

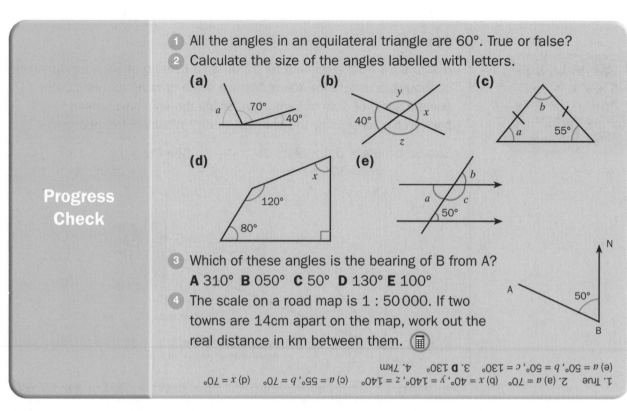

Progress Check

1. All the angles in an equilateral triangle are 60°. True or false?
2. Calculate the size of the angles labelled with letters.

(a)

70°
a
40°

(b)

y
40°
x
z

(c)

b
a 55°

(d)

x
120°
80°

(e)

b
a c
50°

3. Which of these angles is the bearing of B from A?
   A 310° **B** 050° **C** 50° **D** 130° **E** 100°

4. The scale on a road map is 1 : 50 000. If two towns are 14cm apart on the map, work out the real distance in km between them.

N
A
50°
B

1. True   2. (a) $a = 70°$ (b) $x = 40°, y = 140°, z = 140°$ (c) $a = 55°, b = 70°$ (d) $x = 70°$
(e) $a = 50°, b = 50°, c = 130°$ 3. **D** 130°   4. 4.7km

5.3 Pythagoras' theorem

(Level 7) The **hypotenuse** is the longest side of a right-angled triangle. It is always opposite the **right angle**.

Pythagoras' theorem states that:
In any right-angled triangle, the square on the hypotenuse is equal to the sum of the squares on the other two sides.

Key Point

Using the letters in the diagram, the theorem is written as:
$$c^2 = a^2 + b^2$$

This may be rearranged to give:
$$b^2 = c^2 - a^2$$
$$a^2 = c^2 - b^2$$

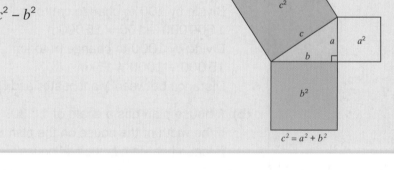

$c^2 = a^2 + b^2$

You need to learn the formula for Pythagoras' theorem. Also learn how it can be rearranged to give the formulae for calculating the lengths of the shorter sides.

Pythagoras' theorem is used to calculate the length of the third side of a right-angled triangle, when the other two sides are known.

Example

Find the length of the missing side in each of these triangles, giving your answer to 1 decimal place.

(a)

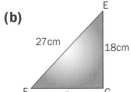

$a^2 = 12^2 + 14.5^2$
$a^2 = 354.25$
$a = \sqrt{354.25}$ ← Square root to find a.
$a = 18.8$m (1 d.p.)

(b)

$27^2 = b^2 + 18^2$
$b^2 = 27^2 - 18^2$
$b^2 = 405$
$b = \sqrt{405}$
$b = 20.1$cm (1 d.p.)

> If you are not told to what degree of accuracy to round, be guided by significant figures given in the question.

Calculating the length of a line segment

(Level 7) You can calculate the length of the line segment joining two points by using Pythagoras' theorem.

For example, by drawing in a triangle between the two points, A(1, 2) and B(7, 6), the length of AB can be found by Pythagoras' theorem.

> The **midpoint** of AB, **M**, can also be found. M has coordinates of (4, 4), i.e. $\left(\frac{1+7}{2}, \frac{2+6}{2}\right)$

Horizontal distance $= 7 - 1 = 6$
Vertical distance $= 6 - 2 = 4$

Length of $(AB)^2 = 6^2 + 4^2$
$(AB)^2 = 36 + 16$
$(AB)^2 = 52$
$AB = \sqrt{52}$
Length of AB $= 7.21$ (2 d.p.)

Solving problems

(Level 7) Pythagoras' theorem can be used to solve practical problems.

Examples

(a) A ladder of length 13m rests against a wall. The ladder reaches 12m up the wall. How far away from the wall is the foot of the ladder?

$13^2 = x^2 + 12^2$
$x^2 = 13^2 - 12^2$
$x^2 = 169 - 144$
$x^2 = 25$
$x = \sqrt{25}$
$x = 5$m

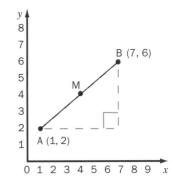

The foot of the ladder is 5m away from the wall.

(b) A cruise liner sets sail from Port A and travels 80km due east then 50km due north, to reach Port B. How far is Port A from Port B by the shortest route?

$a^2 = 80^2 + 50^2$

$a^2 = 6400 + 2500$

$a^2 = 8900$

$a = \sqrt{8900}$

Shortest route = 94.3km (3 s.f.)

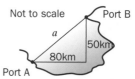

Not to scale   Port B

a

50km

80km

Port A

Progress Check

1 (Level 7) Calculate the lengths of the sides marked with a letter. Give your answers to 1 d.p. 🖩

(a)

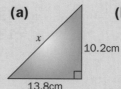

x

10.2cm

13.8cm

(b)

15cm

x

25cm

2 (Level 7) Calculate the height of this isosceles triangle. 🖩

5cm   5cm

3.5cm

3 (Level 7) **(a)** The coordinates of two points are (1, 2) and (7, 10). What is the length of the line joining these two points?

(b) Find the coordinates of the midpoint of the line joining the two points.

1. (a) 17.2cm (b) 20.0cm   2. 4.7cm (1 d.p.)   3. (a) 10 (b) (4, 6)

5.4 Trigonometry in right-angled triangles

Trigonometric ratios

(Level 8) In a right-angled triangle the sides and the angles are related by three trigonometrical ratios: the **sine** (abbreviated to **sin**), the **cosine** (abbreviated to **cos**) and the **tangent** (abbreviated to **tan**).

To use these ratios, you first need to be able to label the sides of the triangle:

Key Point

- **hyp (hypotenuse)** is opposite the right angle.
- **opp (opposite side)** is opposite the angle θ.
- **adj (adjacent side)** is next to the angle θ.

θ is a Greek letter called **theta** and is used to represent angles.

The three trigonometric ratios are:

$\sin \theta = \dfrac{\text{opposite}}{\text{hypotenuse}}$ $\cos \theta = \dfrac{\text{adjacent}}{\text{hypotenuse}}$ $\tan \theta = \dfrac{\text{opposite}}{\text{adjacent}}$

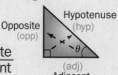

Hypotenuse (hyp)

Opposite (opp)

θ

(adj) Adjacent

The made-up word **SOH CAH TOA** is a quick way of remembering the ratios. The word comes from **S**in equals **O**pposite divided by **H**ypotenuse, etc.

Trigonometry is used to calculate the length of a missing side and the size of a missing angle in right-angled triangles.

Examples

(a) Calculate the length of BC.

Label the sides first.
Decide on the ratio:

$$\sin 30° = \frac{\text{opp}}{\text{hyp}}$$

Substitute in the values:

$$\sin 30° = \frac{BC}{25}$$

$$25 \times \sin 30° = BC$$

$$BC = 12.5\text{cm}$$

(b) Calculate the length of EF.

$$\cos 40° = \frac{\text{adj}}{\text{hyp}} = \frac{20}{EF}$$

EF × cos 40° = 20 ← Multiply both sides by EF.

$$EF = \frac{20}{\cos 40°}$$ ← Divide both sides by cos 40°

$$= 26.1\text{cm (1 d.p.)}$$

Using a calculator key in:

 20 ÷ 40 cos = or 20 ÷ cos 40 =

Check you know how to use your calculator for trig ratios!

(c) Calculate angle ABC.

$$\tan \theta = \frac{\text{opp}}{\text{adj}}$$ ← Label the sides and decide on the ratio.

$$\tan \theta = \frac{15}{27}$$ ← Divide the top value by the bottom value.

$$\tan \theta = 0.\dot{5}$$

$$\theta = \tan^{-1} 0.\dot{5}$$ ← The tan^{-1} shows that we need the angle whose tangent is $0.\dot{5}$

$$\theta = 29°$$ ← To the nearest degree.

To find the angle, you usually use the second function on your calculator.

Solving problems using trigonometry

Trigonometry can be used to solve problems involving right-angled triangles.

Key Point

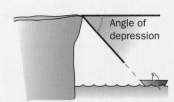

The **angle of elevation** is measured from the horizontal **upwards**.

The **angle of depression** is measured from the horizontal **downwards**.

Examples

(a) Dipak stands 30m from the base of a tower. He measures the angle of elevation from ground level to the top of the tower as 50°. Calculate the height of the tower. Give your answer to 3 s.f.

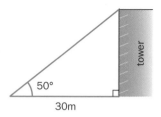

$$\tan 50° = \frac{\text{opp}}{\text{adj}} = \frac{\text{height}}{30}$$

$30 \times \tan 50° = $ height of tower
Height of tower = 35.8m (3 s.f.)

> Make sure you give your answers to the correct degree of accuracy.

(b) Siân is flying a kite. The string is 30m long and is at an angle of 40° to the horizontal. How high is the kite above Siân's head?

$$\sin 40° = \frac{\text{opp}}{\text{hyp}}$$

$$\sin 40° = \frac{a}{30}$$

$30 \times \sin 40° = a$
$a = 19.3$m (3 s.f.)

The kite is 19.3m above Siân's head.

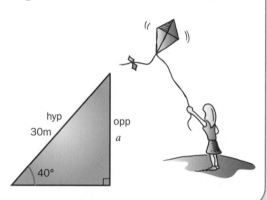

Progress Check

1. **Level 8** Cos 60° = 0.5. True or false? 🖩

2. **Level 8** Calculate the length x in each triangle. 🖩

(a)

40°
12cm
x

(b)

60°
x
9cm

3. **Level 8** Work out the size of the angle θ in each of these triangles. 🖩

(a)

12cm
θ
25cm

(b)

28cm
θ
13cm

4. **Level 8** A circle has a radius of 10cm. Calculate the length of the chord CD. 🖩

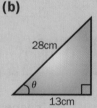

10cm 10cm
120°
C   D

Assessment questions

505

Try the following questions.

Level 4 **1.** Some of these nets can be folded to make cuboids.

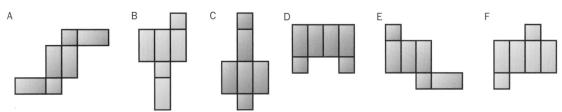

A   B   C   D   E   F

    (a) Which nets can be folded to make a cuboid? _____

    (b) Choose one of the other nets and explain why it cannot be folded to make a cuboid.

_____

Level 5 **2.** The drawing shows an isosceles triangle.

    (a) When angle $s = 50°$, what is the size of angle r? _80_ ✓

    (b) When angle $r = 50°$, what is the size of angle s? _65_ ✓

Level 5 **3.** The scale on a map is 1 : 50 000. Two cities are 15cm away from each other on the map. Work out the actual distance between the two cities in kilometres. 🖩 Ⓒ

_750,000 km._

Level 5 **4.** Hywel shades in a shape made of five squares on a grid.

    (a) Shade in one more square to make a shape with line A as its line of symmetry. Call the square R.

    (b) Going back to the original shape, shade in two more squares to make a shape that has line B as a line of symmetry. Call the squares S and T.

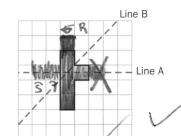

Line B

Line A

Level 5 **5.** For the solid shown, draw:

    (a) the plan

    (b) the view from A

    (c) the view from B

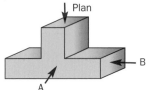

Plan

B

A

a)   b)

Level 6 **6.** The diagram shows a parallelogram. One angle is 52°. Calculate the size of the angle marked p.

_128°_

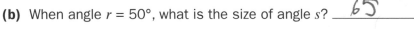

p

52°

Level 6 **7.** Shape A is an equilateral triangle. Continue with the instructions to draw shape A.

    Forward 8

    Turn right 120° ...

forward 8

Turn right 120°

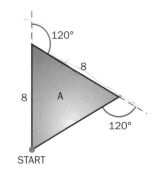

120°

8

8 A

120°

START

625
576

Assessment questions

65 70
45
115

Level 6 **8.** John is drawing some shapes on his computer.
(a) Calculate angles *a*, *b* and *c*.

a=140   b=105   c=115

He then draws a rhombus.
(b) Calculate the size of angles *d* and *e*.

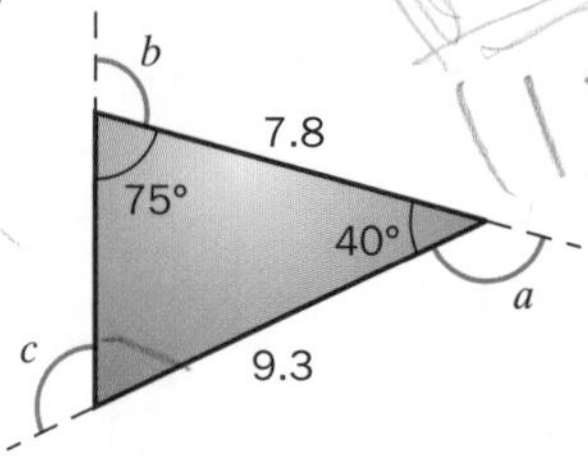

_b_
7.8
75°
40°
_a_
_c_
9.3
12cm
55° _d_
_e_

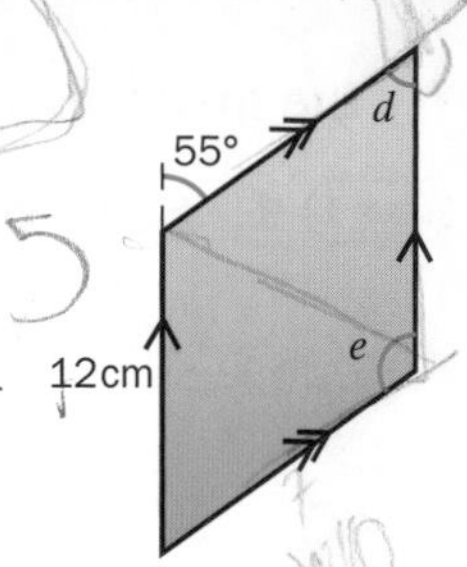

Level 6 **9.** The diagram shows three legs of a cross-country course. The course starts at T, then goes to R and then P, and finally back to T.

(a) Find the bearing of R from T. ____ 110° 15

(b) Find the bearing of R from P. ____

North
P
65
45° R
70°
T

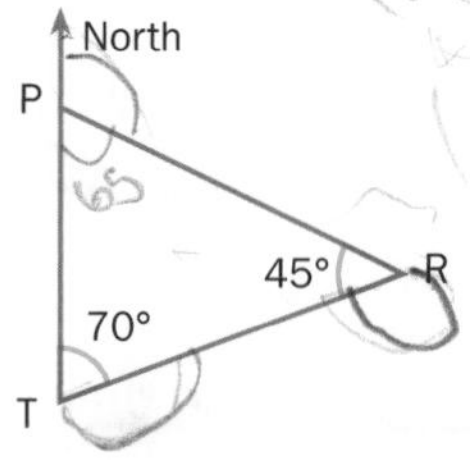

Level 6 **10.** Calculate the size of the interior angle of a regular pentagon.

____

Level 7 **11.** Look at this triangle. Show working to explain why angle *y* must be a right angle.

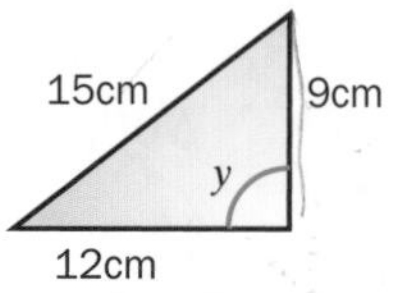

____

15cm   9cm
_y_
12cm

Level 7 **12.** Calculate the area of this triangle.

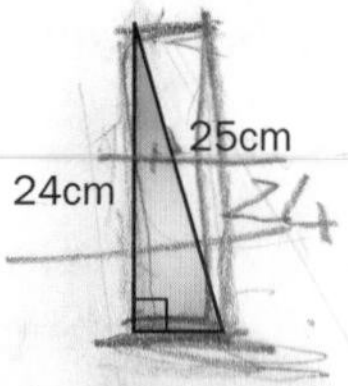

____

24cm 25cm

Level 8 **13.** Seagull Point is 5.2km due north and 8.6km due east of Swamptown.
(a) Calculate the direct distance from Seagull Point to Swamptown.

10.00 km

(b) Daisy wants to sail directly from Swamptown to Seagull Point.
On what bearing should she sail?

NE

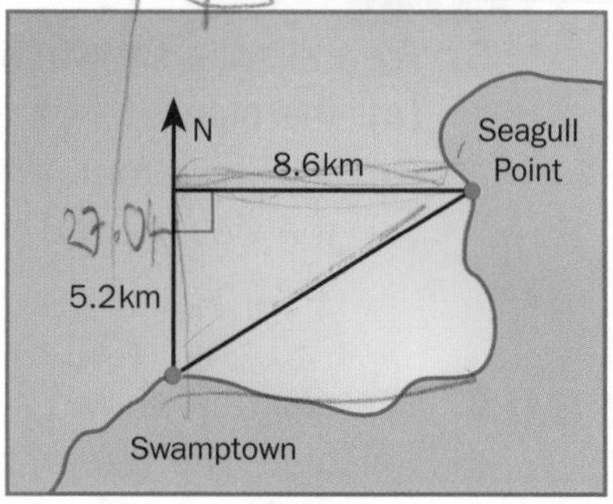

N
8.6km   Seagull Point
5.2km
Swamptown

Level 8 **14.** PQR and PRS are both right-angled triangles.
(a) Calculate the length of PR.

10 cm

(b) Calculate the length of PS.

(c) How much bigger is angle *a* than angle *b*?

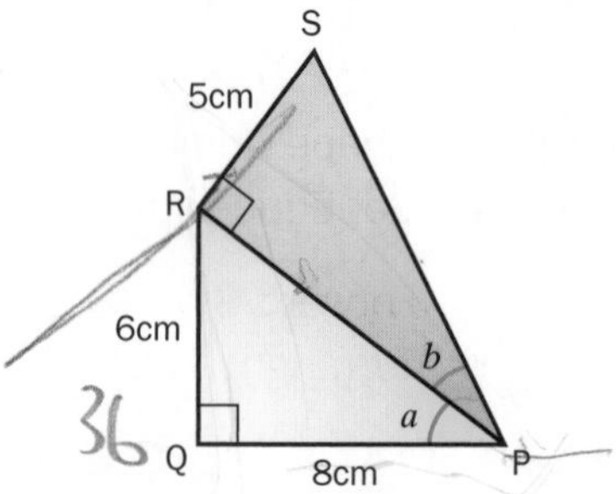

____

S
5cm
R
6cm
36 Q   8cm   P
_b_ _a_
64

Transformations, constructions and loci

After studying this section you should be able to:

- transform 2-D shapes using translation, reflection and rotation
- enlarge 2-D shapes given a centre of enlargement and a positive scale factor
- transform 2-D shapes by combinations of translations, reflections and rotations
- recognise and use similarity to solve problems
- make constructions and draw loci

6.1 Transformations and similarity

3 16.333
9Tu

A transformation changes the position or size of a shape. There are four types of transformation: **translation**, **reflection**, **rotation** and **enlargement**.

Reflections and translations

A **reflection** creates an image of an object on the other side of a **mirror line**. The mirror line is known as an **axis of reflection**. The size and shape of the figure are not changed. Understanding reflections and translations helps us to appreciate patterns in nature.

A reflection that maps A to A' also maps A' to A, i.e. reflection is a **self-inverse** transformation. The mirror line is the **perpendicular bisector** of the line joining A to its image A'.

24

Examples

(a) Reflect triangle ABC in the mirror line. Plot the image points first. They are the same distance from the mirror line as the object. Join up the image points.

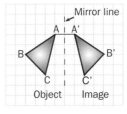

(b) Reflect triangle ABC in:
 (i) the x-axis and label it D
 (ii) the line $y = -x$ and label it E
 (iii) the line $x = 5$ and label it F.

Triangles D, E and F are **congruent** to triangle ABC.

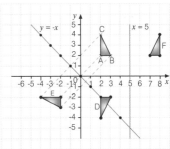

(Level 8) A **translation** moves objects from one place to another. The size and shape of the object are not changed. **Vectors** are used to describe the distance and direction of the translation.

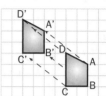

Examples

(a) Draw the image of ABCD after a translation of 4 squares to the left and 3 squares up.

ABCD and A'B'C'D' are congruent.

(b) (i) Translate ABC by the vector $\binom{2}{1}$ and label it P.

(ii) Translate ABC by the vector $\binom{-3}{-2}$ and label it Q.

Triangles ABC, P and Q are all congruent.

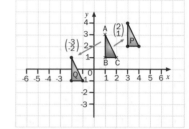

> A vector is written as $\binom{a}{b}$.
> a represents the **horizontal** movement.
> b represents the **vertical** movement.

Rotations

Rotations turn an object through an angle about some fixed point. This fixed point is called the **centre of rotation**. The size or shape of the object is not changed.

To describe a rotation, give three pieces of information:
- The centre of rotation
- The direction of rotation (clockwise or anticlockwise)
- The angle of rotation

For example, this is a 90° rotation about 0, in a clockwise direction (also known as a $\frac{1}{4}$ turn clockwise).

> By convention, an anticlockwise rotation is positive and a clockwise rotation is negative.

Example

Rotate triangle ABC:
(a) 90° clockwise about (0, 0) and label it R.
(b) 180° about (0, 0) and label it S.
(c) 90° anticlockwise about (-1, 1) and label it T.

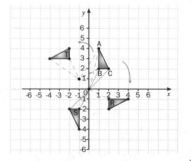

Enlargements

Enlargements change the size but not the shape of the object. The **centre of enlargement** is the point from which the enlargement takes place. The **scale factor** (k) indicates how many times the length of the original figure has changed. Enlargement with a scale factor k makes the lengths k times longer:

- If the scale factor is **greater than 1**, the object becomes **bigger**.
- If the scale factor is **less than 1**, the object becomes **smaller**.
- (Level 7) A negative scale factor places the image on the opposite side of the centre of enlargement to the object.

Examples

(a) Enlarge triangle ABC by a scale factor of 2, centre (0, 0). Label the image A'B'C'.

Notice that each side of the enlargement is twice the size of the original. OC' = 2 × OC.

(b) (Level 7) Enlarge triangle ABC by a scale factor -$\frac{1}{2}$, centre (0, 0). Label the image A"B"C".

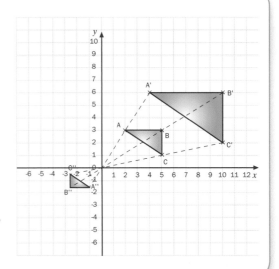

> When asked to describe an enlargement, you must include the scale factor and the position of the centre of enlargement.

(Level 7) ABC has been enlarged with a scale factor $\frac{1}{2}$, to give A'B'C'. The centre of enlargement is at O.
The length of OA' is $\frac{1}{2}$OA.

The terms multiplication and enlargement are still used even when the scale factor (or multiplier) is less than 1.

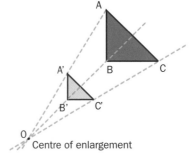

Key Point

Two successive enlargements with scale factors k_1 and k_2 are equivalent to a single enlargement with scale factor $k_1 \times k_2$.

Combining transformations

Examples

(a) Reflect ABC in the x-axis. Label the image $A_1B_1C_1$.
(b) Reflect $A_1B_1C_1$ in the y-axis. Label the image $A_2B_2C_2$.

The single transformation that maps ABC directly onto $A_2B_2C_2$ is a rotation of 180°, centre (0, 0).

> Some computer packages are useful when doing transformations.

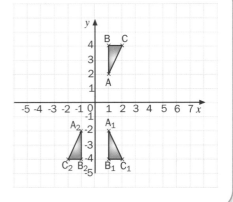

Similar figures

Key Point

(Level 8) Similar figures are the **same shape** but **different sizes**. (Shapes that have been enlarged are similar.) Corresponding **angles** are **equal**. Corresponding **lengths** are in the **same ratio**.

For example:

Corresponding angles are equal.

Since corresponding lengths are in the same ratio, missing lengths of similar figures can be found.

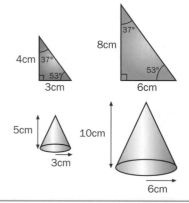

Example

Find the missing length a, giving your answer to 2 s.f.

9cm   14cm a 11cm

$\dfrac{a}{11} = \dfrac{9}{14}$ ◄— Corresponding sides are in the same ratio.

$a = \dfrac{9}{14} \times 11$ ◄— Multiply both sides by 11.

$a = 7.1\text{cm (2 s.f.)}$

Progress Check

1. On the diagram:
   (a) translate ABC by the vector $\begin{pmatrix} -3 \\ 1 \end{pmatrix}$. Label it P.
   (b) reflect ABC in the line $y = x$. Label it Q.
   (c) reflect ABC in the line $y = -1$. Label it R.
   (d) rotate ABC 180° about (0, 0). Label it S.

2. (Level 7) A shape is enlarged with a scale factor of 3, followed by an enlargement with scale factor 2. How many times longer is the final image than the original shape?
   A 2 **B** 3 **C** 5 **D** 6 **E** 12

3. (Level 8) The two cylinders are similar. Work out the value of x. 🖩

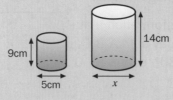

9cm   14cm   5cm x

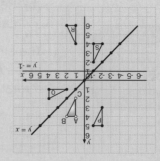

3. 7.8cm
2. **D** 6
1. (a)–(d)

6.2 Constructions and loci

You need to know how to construct the following, using a compass and a ruler. It is often helpful to make a sketch diagram first.

Triangle

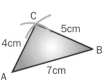

To construct a triangle:
- Draw the longest side.
- With the compass point at A, draw an arc of radius 4cm.
- With the compass point at B, draw an arc of radius 5cm.
- Join A and B to the point where the two arcs meet.

The perpendicular bisector of a line

- Draw a line XY.
- Draw two arcs with the compass, using X as the centre. The compass must be set at a radius greater than half the distance of XY.
- Draw two more arcs with Y as the centre (keep the compass the same distance apart as before).
- Join the two points where the arcs cross.
- AB is the **perpendicular bisector** of XY.
- N is the **midpoint** of XY.

The perpendicular from a point to a line

- From P draw arcs to cut the line at A and B.
- From A and B draw arcs with the same radius to intersect at C.
- Join P to C; this line is perpendicular to the line AB.

To bisect an angle

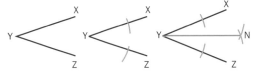

- Draw two lines XY and YZ to meet at an angle.
- Using a compass, place the point at Y and draw two arcs on XY and YZ.
- Place the compass point at the two arcs on XY and YZ and draw arcs to cross at N. Join Y to N. YN is the **bisector** of angle XYZ.

The perpendicular from a point on a straight line

Practise drawing these constructions. Do not rub out your construction lines when drawn.

- With a compass set to a radius of several cm, and centred on N, draw arcs to cut the line at A and B.
- Construct the perpendicular bisector of the line segment AB as shown above.

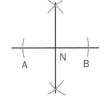

Locus

Key Point

(Level 7) The **locus** of a point is the set of all the possible positions which that point can occupy, subject to some given conditions or rules. The plural of locus is **loci**.

- The locus of the points that are a constant distance from a fixed point is a circle.

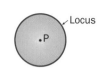

- The locus of the points that are equidistant from two points X and Y is the perpendicular bisector of XY.

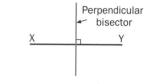

- The locus of the points that are equidistant from two lines is the line that bisects the angle between the lines.

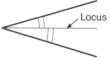

- The locus of the points that are a constant distance from a line is a pair of parallel lines above and below the line. (Remember that a line is infinitely long.)

For a line segment, there would be semicircles on either end.

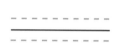

Examples

(a) Two radio stations A and B, 80km apart, broadcast over distances of 50 and 60km respectively. Using a scale of 1cm = 20km, show the area where both stations can be heard.

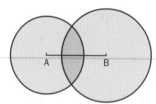

These diagrams are not to scale. (In an assessment you would be expected to draw scale diagrams.)

The darker-shaded region represents the required area.

(b) The diagram shows a rectangular field. Gertie the goat can only eat grass in the area that satisfies these given conditions:
- Not more than 2m from P
- At least 3.5m away from the wall QR. (Scale 1cm = 1m)

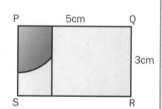

The green-shaded region shows where Gertie can eat the grass.

Progress Check

1 (Level 7) A gold coin is buried in a rectangular field. It is 4m from T and equidistant from RU and RS.
Mark with an X the position of the gold coin.
(Note: draw the rectangle with a scale of 1cm = 1m.)

2 Draw an angle of 40°. Bisect the angle accurately, showing all construction lines.

3 Construct the perpendicular bisector of a 10cm line AB.

2. The angle must be drawn accurately to 40° (±1°) and construction lines shown for the bisector.

1. (Diagram not to scale. In an assessment you would be expected to draw a scale diagram.)

Assessment questions

Try the following questions.

(Level 6) **1.** Use a compass to construct an isosceles triangle. One side must be 5cm, another side must be 7cm. Construct accurately two different isosceles triangles.

(Level 6) **2.** The grid shows two 'T' shapes.
The bigger 'T' shape is an enlargement of the smaller 'T' shape.
(a) What is the scale factor of the enlargement? _____
(b) On the grid, show where the centre of enlargement is by marking the correct place with a cross.

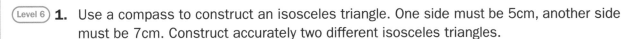

(Level 6) **3.** **(a)** You can rotate triangle A onto triangle B. Put a cross on the centre of rotation.
(b) Triangle B can be rotated anticlockwise onto triangle A. What is the angle of rotation?

_____

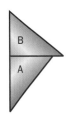

(Level 6) **4.** **(a)** Reflect triangle A in the mirror line.

(b) (i) Translate triangle B 4 squares to the right and 2 squares downwards.
(ii) Write down the vector that represents the translation in (i). _____

Mirror line

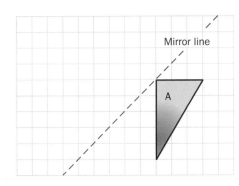

A

B

(Level 6) **5.** Heather wants to make a cuboid twice as long, twice as high and twice as wide as this cuboid. How many small cubes will she need altogether?

_____

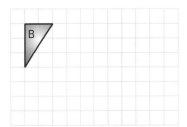

(Level 6) **6.** **(a)** Rotate the 'L' shape 90° anticlockwise about the point A. Label it R.
(b) Rotate the 'L' shape 180° clockwise about the point A. Label it T.

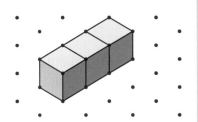

(Level 6) **7.** Enlarge shape P with a scale factor of 3.

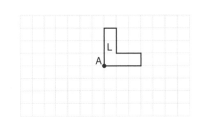

Assessment questions

Level 7 **8.** The plan shows the position of three towns, each marked with a cross. The scale of the plan is 1cm to 10km. The towns need a new television mast. The new TV mast must be: nearer to Acton than Cecilton and less than 55km from Brownton. On a separate 5mm squared piece of paper, show the region where the new television mast can be placed. (Leave in your construction lines.)

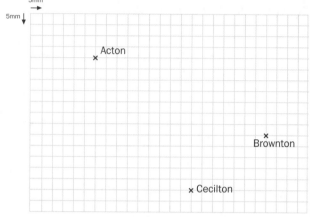

Level 7 **9.** Emily is redesigning her garden. She wishes to plant a tree in the garden. The tree must be at least 4m from the house and at least 10m from the centre of the pond. Show accurately the region in which the tree can be planted.

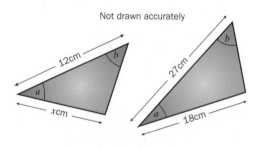

SCALE: 1cm to 4m

Level 8 **10.** These plant pots are similar. The internal dimensions are shown. Calculate the height *p*. 🖩

_____

_____

_____

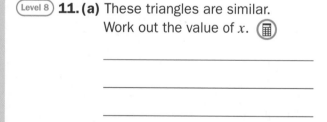

Not to scale

Level 8 **11. (a)** These triangles are similar. Work out the value of *x*. 🖩

_____

_____

_____

Not drawn accurately

(b) Look at these triangles. Are they similar? Explain your answer.

_____

_____

_____

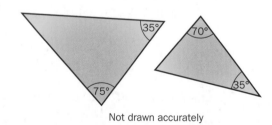

Not drawn accurately

7 Measures and measurement

Learning Summary

After studying this section you should be able to:

- interpret numbers on a range of measuring instruments, and choose and use appropriate units
- use metric and imperial units, and solve problems involving the conversion of units
- find the area and perimeter of 2-D shapes
- know and use the formulae for the circumference and area of a circle
- calculate the volume of a variety of 3-D solids
- understand the difference between formulae for perimeter, area and volume by considering dimensions

7.1 Units of measurement

Estimating

Estimating is a useful skill in everyday life. Some of the measures that you need to be able to estimate are:

Length	Capacity	Weight	Time

For example:

- A door is about 2m high.

- A can of soft drink holds about 330ml or $\frac{1}{2}$ pint.

- A bag of sugar holds 1kg or about 2.2lb.

Metric units

Metric units include **kilometres** (km), **metres** (m), **kilograms** (kg), **litres** (l), etc.

Length	Weight	Capacity
10mm = 1cm	1000mg = 1g	1000ml = 1 litre
100cm = 1m	1000g = 1kg	100cl = 1 litre
1000m = 1km	1000kg = 1 tonne	1000cm³ = 1 litre

Key Point

Remember the following when converting units:
- If changing from **small** units **to large** units, you **divide** (e.g. g → kg).
- If changing from **large** units **to small** units, you **multiply** (e.g. m → cm).

When converting one unit to another, try to decide first whether your answer will be larger or smaller, then multiply or divide as appropriate.

For example:
500cm = 5m (÷ 100)
5 litres = 500cl (× 100)
3500g = 3.5kg (÷ 1000)
25cm = 250mm (× 10)

These diagrams may help you to remember:

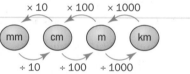 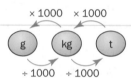 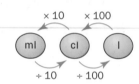

Imperial units

Imperial units include **miles**, **yards**, **stones**, **pints**, etc. They are sometimes thought of as the 'old fashioned' units of measurement.

Length	Weight	Capacity
1 foot = 12 inches	1 stone = 14 pounds (lb)	20 fluid oz = 1 pint
1 yard = 3 feet	1 pound = 16 ounces (oz)	8 pints = 1 gallon

Here are some approximate comparisons between metric and imperial units.

Length	Weight	Capacity
2.5cm ≈ 1 inch	25g ≈ 1 ounce	1 litre ≈ $1\frac{3}{4}$ pints
30cm ≈ 1 foot	1kg ≈ 2.2 pounds	4.5 litres ≈ 1 gallon
1m ≈ 39 inches		
8km ≈ 5 miles		

Examples

(a) Change 25km into miles.

8km ≈ 5 miles so 1km ≈ $\frac{5}{8}$ mile.

25km ≈ 25 × $\frac{5}{8}$ = 15.6 miles (1 d.p.)

(b) A plate is 6 inches across. Roughly how many centimetres is this?

2.5cm ≈ 1 inch   6 inches ≈ 6 × 2.5 = 15cm

Choosing the correct units of measurement

When you want to measure something, it is important that sensible units are used.

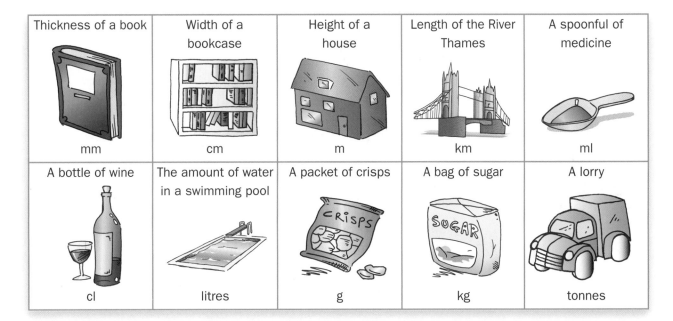

Thickness of a book	Width of a bookcase	Height of a house	Length of the River Thames	A spoonful of medicine
mm	cm	m	km	ml
A bottle of wine	The amount of water in a swimming pool	A packet of crisps	A bag of sugar	A lorry
cl	litres	g	kg	tonnes

Time measurement

Of all the measurements used in everyday life, **time** is probably used most often. You need to be able to tell the difference between times in the morning and times in the afternoon and evening.

Time can be measured using the 12 or 24-hour clock. The **12-hour clock** uses am and pm. Times before midday are am, and times after midday are pm. The **24-hour clock** numbers the hours from 0 to 24. Times are written with four figures.

For example:
- 2.42pm is the same as 1442
- 3.30am is the same as 0330
- 1527 is the same as 3.27pm
- 0704 is the same as 7.04am

Units of time

There are 60 seconds in one minute.
There are 60 minutes in one hour.
There are 24 hours in one day.
There are seven days in one week.
There are 52 weeks in one year.
There are 365 days in a year, or 366 in a leap year.

This clock reads 10 past 7. The short hand tells us the hour, and the long hand tells us the minutes.

Timetables

24-hour clock times often appear on bus and train timetables.

> **Example**
>
> The train timetable gives the times from London to Manchester.
>
> | | | | | | |
> |---|---|---|---|---|---|
> | London Euston | 0702 | 0740 | Every 60 | 1100 | 1400 |
> | Watford Junction | 0732 | 0812 | minutes | 1130 | 1430 |
> | Stoke-on-Trent | 0850 | 0930 | until | - | 1545 |
> | Manchester Piccadilly | 0940 | 1015 | | 1315 | 1640 |
>
> The 0850 train from Stoke-on-Trent   The 0740 train from London Euston arrives at 1015   The 1100 train from London Euston does not stop at Stoke-on-Trent
>
> **(a)** Diana is travelling from Watford Junction to Manchester Piccadilly. If she catches the 0732 train from Watford, how long is her journey?
>
> Departs Watford: 0732   Arrives Manchester: 0940
> Time = 2 hours 8 minutes
>
> **(b)** Sebastian arrives at London Euston at 1242. How long does he have to wait for the next train to Manchester?
>
> 1242 → 1300 = 18 minutes ⎫
> 1300 → 1400 = 1 hour   ⎬ Waiting time is 1 hour 18 minutes

Compound measures

This can be used to help remember the formulae.

Level 7 **Speed** can be measured in kilometres per hour (km/h), miles per hour (mph) and metres per second (m/s). These are all **compound measures** because they involve a combination of two basic measures. **Density** and **pressure** are also examples of compound measures.

The abbreviation for 'per' is a 'p' or '/' and is used to mean 'for every' or 'in every', e.g. mph (miles travelled in every hour).

Key Point

Average speed = $\dfrac{\text{total distance travelled}}{\text{total time taken}} = \dfrac{d}{t}$

From this speed formula two others can be obtained:

Time = $\dfrac{\text{distance}}{\text{speed}}$ Distance = speed × time

Examples

(a) Lynette walks 10km in 4 hours. Find her average speed.

$$s = \frac{d}{t}$$

$$s = \frac{10}{4} = 2.5\text{km/h}$$

Notice the units.

(b) Mr Rosenthal drove a distance of 250 miles at an average speed of 70 miles per hour. How long did the journey take?

$$t = \frac{d}{s} \qquad \therefore t = \frac{250}{70} = 3.57 \text{ hours}$$

3.57h must be changed into hours and minutes. To do this:
- subtract the hours
- multiply the decimal part by 60, i.e. 0.57... × 60 = 34min (nearest minute).

Journey time = 3h 34min

Key Point

To calculate density, volume and mass, use:

$$\text{Density} = \frac{\text{mass}}{\text{volume}}, \quad D = \frac{M}{V} \qquad \text{Volume} = \frac{M}{D} \qquad \text{Mass} = D \times V$$

can be used.

Example

Find the density of an object whose mass is 600g and whose volume is 50cm³.

$$\text{Density} = \frac{M}{V} = \frac{600}{50} = 12\text{g/cm}^3$$

Key Point

To calculate pressure use:

$$\text{Pressure} = \frac{\text{force on surface}}{\text{surface area}}, \quad p = \frac{f}{a}$$

Progress Check

1. Approximately how many pounds are in 2kg of sugar?
2. For each of these statements write down whether it is true or false.
   (a) Metres are used to measure the length of a car.
   (b) Grams are used to measure the thickness of a pane of glass.
   (c) Litres are used to measure the capacity of a large bottle of fizzy drink.
3. Change 5 litres into ml.
4. Change 5 inches into cm.
5. 3.30am written in 24-hour clock time is which of the following?
   A 0330   **B** 3.30   **C** 1530   **D** 330
6. (Level 7) The mass of an object is 500g. If its density is 6.2g/cm³, what is the volume of the object?

6. 80.65cm³ (2 d.p.)
1. 4.4lb   2. (a) True (b) False (c) True   3. 5000ml   4. 12.5cm   5. A 0330

7.2 Area and perimeter of 2-D shapes

Estimating areas of 2-D shapes

Key Point

The distance around the outside edge of a shape is called the **perimeter**.

The **area** of a 2-D shape is the amount of space it covers. Units of area are mm², cm² and m².

Areas of irregular shapes can be found by counting the squares the shape covers.

Label the squares as you count them. Try to match up parts of squares to make a whole one.

Examples

(a) Find the area of this shape.

This shape has an area of about 20.5 square units.

These make one whole square

This is half a square

(b) Find the perimeter of this shape.

Perimeter = 4 + 5 + 3 + 2.7 + 2.7
= 17.4cm

Areas of quadrilaterals and triangles

Learn the formulae for these 2-D shapes.

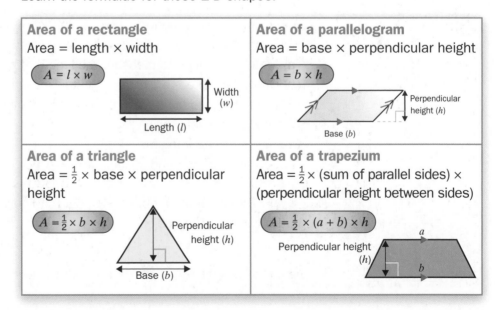

Area of a rectangle
Area = length × width

$A = l \times w$

Width (w)

Length (l)

Area of a parallelogram
Area = base × perpendicular height

$A = b \times h$

Perpendicular height (h)

Base (b)

Area of a triangle
Area = ½ × base × perpendicular height

$A = \frac{1}{2} \times b \times h$

Perpendicular height (h)

Base (b)

Area of a trapezium
Area = ½ × (sum of parallel sides) × (perpendicular height between sides)

$A = \frac{1}{2} \times (a + b) \times h$

Perpendicular height (h)

a

b

Examples

(a) Find the area of the following shapes, giving your answers to 3 s.f. where necessary.

(i)

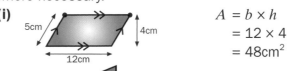

5cm   4cm
12cm

$A = b \times h$
$\quad = 12 \times 4$
$\quad = 48\text{cm}^2$

(ii)

4.9cm   10.1cm
6.2cm

$A = \frac{1}{2} \times (a + b) \times h$
$\quad = \frac{1}{2} \times (4.9 + 10.1) \times 6.2$
$\quad = 46.5\text{cm}^2$

(iii)

① 4.7cm
② 5.5cm
← 12.3cm →

> Split the shape into two parts and find the areas of each.

Area of ① $= \frac{1}{2} \times b \times h$
$\qquad = \frac{1}{2} \times 12.3 \times 4.7$
$\qquad = 28.905\text{cm}^2$

Area of ② $= b \times h$
$\qquad = 12.3 \times 5.5$
$\qquad = 67.65\text{cm}^2$

> Notice that rounding does not take place until the end.

Total area $=$ ① $+$ ②
$\qquad = 28.905 + 67.65$
$\qquad = 96.555$
$\qquad = 96.6\text{cm}^2$ (3 s.f.)

(b) If the area of this triangle is 55cm², find the height giving your answer to 3 s.f.

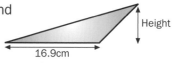

Height
16.9cm

$A = \frac{1}{2} \times b \times h$
$55 = \frac{1}{2} \times 16.9 \times h$ ← Substitute values into the formula.
$55 = 8.45 \times h$
$h = \dfrac{55}{8.45}$ ← Divide both sides by 8.45
$h = 6.51\text{cm}$ (3 s.f.)

Circumference and area of a circle

Key Point

Circumference $= \pi \times$ diameter $\qquad C = \pi \times d$
$\qquad\qquad\quad = 2 \times \pi \times$ radius $\qquad C = 2 \times \pi \times r$
Area $= \pi \times (\text{radius})^2 \qquad A = \pi \times r^2$

Radius
Diameter
O

> It is important that you remember these formulae.

Examples

(a) Find the circumference and area of this circle. Use $\pi = 3.142$

$C = \pi \times d$
$C = 3.142 \times 10$
$C = 31.42\text{cm}$

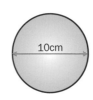

10cm

> Halve the diameter to obtain the radius.

$A = \pi \times r^2$
$A = 3.142 \times 5^2$
$A = 78.55\text{cm}^2$

(b) A circular fish pond has a circumference of 12m. Work out the length of the diameter to 1 d.p. Use $\pi = 3.142$

$$C = \pi \times d$$
$$12 = 3.142 \times d$$
$$\frac{12}{3.142} = d$$

So $d = 3.8192...$ $d = 3.8$m (1 d.p.)

(c) A circular flower bed has an area of 1256m². Work out its radius. Use $\pi = 3.14$

$$A = \pi \times r^2$$
$$1256 = 3.14 \times r^2$$
$$\frac{1256}{3.14} = r^2 \quad \longleftarrow \boxed{\text{Divide both sides by 3.14}}$$
$$r^2 = 400$$
$$r = \sqrt{400} \quad \longleftarrow \boxed{\text{Square root to obtain the radius.}}$$
$$r = 20\text{m}$$

(Level 8) When finding an **arc length** or a **sector area** of a circle, it is important to remember that they are just a fraction of the circumference or the area of the circle.

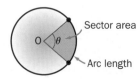

$$\text{Arc length} = \frac{\theta}{360°} \times \pi \times d \qquad \text{Sector area} = \frac{\theta}{360°} \times \pi \times r^2$$

where θ is the size of the angle between the two bounding radii.

Areas of enlarged shapes

(Level 7) A common mistake is to assume that an enlargement with scale factor 3 makes the area 3× larger. In fact, the area of the image is 9× the area of the original shape.

Key Point

If a shape is **enlarged** by a **scale factor** n, then the **area** of the enlarged shape is n^2 **times bigger**.

For example, if $n = 2$:
- the length of the enlarged shape is twice as big
- the area of the enlarged shape becomes four times as big (i.e. $2^2 = 4$).

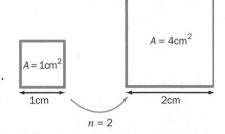

Changing area units

Key Point

(Level 7) $1\text{m}^2 = 10\,000\text{cm}^2$

For example:
This square has a length of 1 metre.
This is the same as a length of 100cm.
Hence $1m^2 = 100 \times 100cm^2$
$\qquad 1m^2 = 10\,000cm^2$

Always check that the measurements are in the same units before you calculate an area.

1 Work out the areas of the following shapes, giving your answers to 3 s.f. Use the π key on your calculator.

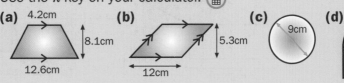

(a) 4.2cm / 8.1cm / 12.6cm **(b)** 5.3cm / 12cm **(c)** 9cm **(d)** 8cm / 15cm

2 Work out the area of the region shaded green. Use the π key on your calculator.

←10cm→

3 (Level 7) Change $5m^2$ to cm^2. Which answer is correct?
A $5000cm^2$ **B** $500cm^2$ **C** $50\,000cm^2$ **D** $500\,000cm^2$

4 Fill in the gap.
A circle of area $100cm^2$ has a radius of _____(1 d.p.). (Use π = 3.142)

1. (a) $68.0cm^2$ (3 s.f.) (b) $63.6cm^2$ (3 s.f.) (c) $63.6cm^2$ (3 s.f.) (d) $208cm^2$ (3 s.f.)
2. $21.5cm^2$ (3 s.f.) 3. **C** $50\,000cm^2$ 4. 5.6cm (1 d.p.)

7.3 Volume of 3-D solids

The volume of a 3-D solid is the amount of space it occupies.
Units of volume are mm^3, cm^3 and m^3.

Key Point

The volume of a 3-D solid can be found by counting the number of $1cm^3$ cubes.

For example:
The volume of the solid opposite is $24cm^3$.

Each cube has a volume of $1cm^3$
(1 cubic centimetre).

1cm
1cm
1cm

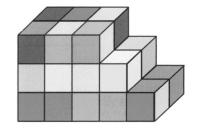

Calculating volume and surface area

Key Point	A **prism** is any solid which can be cut into slices that are all the same shape. A prism has a **uniform cross-section**.

Volume of a cuboid
Volume = length × width × height
$$V = l \times w \times h$$

Volume of a prism
Volume = area of cross-section × length
$$V = A \times l$$

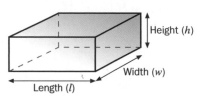

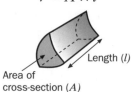

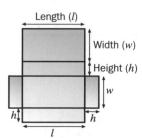

Surface area = the sum of the areas of the faces
Surface area of a cuboid
$$= 2 \times l \times h + 2 \times w \times h + 2 \times w \times l$$

> Two faces have area $l \times h$

(Level 7) **Volume of a cylinder**

Cylinders are prisms whose cross-section is a circle.
Volume = area of cross-section × length
$$V = \pi r^2 \times h$$

> Area of circle   Height or length

Surface area of a cylinder = $2\pi r^2 + 2\pi rh$

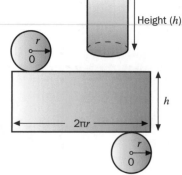

Examples

(a) Look at the cuboid opposite.
  (i) Work out the volume of the cuboid.

Volume = $l \times w \times h$
= $10 \times 8 \times 2 = 160\text{cm}^3$

(ii) The cuboid contains a present. Work out the amount of paper needed to wrap the present assuming there is no overlap.

Surface area = 2 × (face A + face B + face C)
Face A = $10 \times 2 = 20\text{cm}^2$
Face B = $8 \times 2 = 16\text{cm}^2$
Face C = $10 \times 8 = 80\text{cm}^2$
Total amount of paper needed = 2 × (20 + 16 + 80)
= 2 × 116 = 232cm^2

> Make sure that you show full working out.

(b) The cross-section of a solid is in the shape of a trapezium. Work out the volume of the solid.

Area of cross-section:
$A = \frac{1}{2} \times (a + b) \times h$

$A = \frac{1}{2} \times (3 + 8) \times 5 = 27.5 \text{cm}^2$

Volume = 27.5 × 4
        = 110cm³

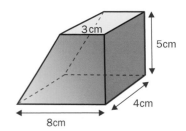

(c) Cat food is sold in tins. Work out the following using $\pi = 3.142$
  (i) The volume of cat food that the tin contains.

$V = \pi \times r^2 \times h$
$V = 3.142 \times 4^2 \times 10$
$V = 502.72$
$V = 503\text{cm}^3$ (3 s.f.)

> Remember to put units in your answer.

(ii) The total area of metal needed to make the tin.

Total area of metal = $2\pi r^2 + 2\pi rh$
$A = 2 \times 3.142 \times 4^2 + 2 \times 3.142 \times 4 \times 10$
$A = 100.544 + 251.36$
$A = 351.904$
$A = 352\text{cm}^2$ (3 s.f.)

Volumes of enlarged solids

Key Point

(Level 7) If a solid is enlarged by a **scale factor** n, the **volume** of the enlarged solid is n^3 **times bigger.**

For example:
If a cube of length 1cm is enlarged by a scale factor of 2, the volume of the enlarged cube is eight times bigger ($2^3 = 8$).

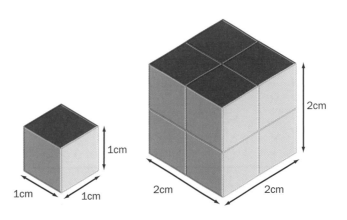

Converting volume units

(Level 7) $1m^3 = 1\,000\,000cm^3$

It is better to change all the lengths to the same unit before starting a question.

For example:
This cube has a length of 1m. This is the same as a length of 100cm.

Hence $1m^3 = 100 \times 100 \times 100cm^3$
$= 1\,000\,000cm^3$

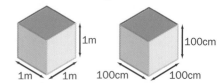

Dimensions

Key Point

(Level 7) The dimension of perimeter is length (L); it is measured in one dimension.

The dimension of area is length × length ($L \times L = L^2$); it is a measurement in two dimensions.

The dimension of volume is length × length × length ($L \times L \times L = L^3$); it is a measurement in three dimensions.

Example

The letters a, b, c and d all represent lengths. For each formula write down whether it represents a length, area or volume.

(a) $a^2b = (L \times L \times L) =$ volume

(b) $\dfrac{2\pi ab}{d} = \dfrac{L \times L}{L} =$ length

2 and π are constants so they have no dimensions. We just ignore them.

(c) $a^2 + 4cd = L \times L + L \times L =$ area

A formula with a mixed dimension is impossible, e.g. $L^3 + L^2$.

Progress Check

1. Work out the volumes of the following solids to 3 s.f. 📱

   (a)

   6.5cm

   19.8cm

   27.2cm

   (b)

   85cm

   10.6cm

2. Work out the surface area of a cuboid with height 6cm, width 4cm and length 10cm.

3. (Level 7) The volume of a cylinder is $2000cm^3$ and its radius is 5.6cm. Work out its height to 3 s.f. Use the π key on your calculator. 📱

4. (Level 7) A prism has a volume of $10cm^3$. The prism is enlarged by a scale factor of 3. What is the volume of the enlarged prism?
   A $90cm^3$ **B** $27cm^3$ **C** $270cm^3$ **D** $900cm^3$ **E** $30cm^3$

1. (a) 1750cm³ (3 s.f.) (b) 60 100cm³ (3 s.f.) 2. 248cm² 3. 20.3cm (3 s.f.) 4. **C** 270cm³

Assessment questions

Try the following questions.

Level 4 **1.** For the shape opposite drawn on a 1cm grid, write down:
    (a) the area of the shape _____
    (b) the perimeter of the shape. _____

Level 5 **2.** The following information shows how long it takes to fly between some cities.

From	To	Time
London	Paris	1 hour 15 minutes
London	Tokyo	12 hours 40 minutes
Paris	Sydney	22 hours 10 minutes
Tokyo	Sydney	9 hours 15 minutes

    (a) Bina flies from London to Paris and then from Paris to Sydney.
         How long is the flight time in total?_____
    (b) Jessica leaves Tokyo at 1800.
         What time will it be in Tokyo when she is due to land in Sydney? _____

Level 5 **3.** I need exactly 2 litres of orange juice. I have a measuring jug that holds
800ml when full.
Explain how I can use my measuring jug to obtain 2 litres of orange juice.

_____

Level 5 **4.** **(a)** Arrange these lengths in order of size.

      (5 kilometres) (5 centimetres) (5 miles) (5 metres) _____

    (b) Arrange these masses in order of size.

      (2 grams) (2 milligrams) (2 pounds) (2 kilograms) _____

Level 5 **5.** How many kilometres are there in 15 miles? _____

Level 6 **6.** Each shape has an area of 100cm² and a vertical height of 5cm. Calculate the length of
the base. 🖩
    (a)

                 5cm

         ?

    (b) 18cm
                    5cm

         ?

Level 6 **7.** The diagram shows the plan of a room. Carpet is being laid
on the floor. 1m² of carpet costs £35.99. Work out the total
cost of carpeting the room. 🖩 _____

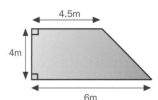

Level 6 **8.** The diagram shows the plan of a rectangular garden.
A circular pond is in the garden. What percentage of the
area of the garden is taken up by the pond? Use the
π key on your calculator. Give your answer to 1 d.p. 🖩

_____

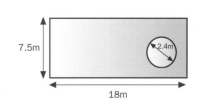

Assessment questions

(Level 6) **9.** Hannah wants to paint the outside walls, roof and door of her shed (shown opposite) with wood preservative. The shed does not have any windows. A tin of wood preservative costs £8.75 and covers 20m². Work out how much it will cost Hannah to paint all four walls, the roof and door of her shed.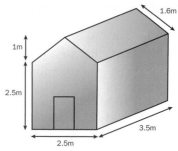

_____

(Level 7) **10.** Audrey said, 'There are 100 square centimetres in a square metre.' Audrey is wrong. Explain why she is wrong.

_____

(Level 7) **11.** The volume of a cylinder is 300cm³. If the height of the cylinder is 15cm, calculate the radius. Use π = 3.142 and give your answer to 1 d.p.

_____

(Level 7) **12.** TC dog food is in tins in the shape of cylinders. The internal measurements of the tin are shown. Use the π key on your calculator for the following:

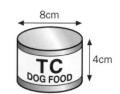

(a) Work out the volume of the tin. _____

(b) The label that goes around the tin fits exactly. Work out the area of paper that is needed to make the label.

_____

(Level 8) (c) The makers of TC dog food decide to make larger tins. Each dimension is multiplied by 3. Explain why the volume of the new tins is now 27 times greater than the volume of the original tins.

_____

(Level 8) **13.** The solid is a prism with height 5x. Write an expression for the volume of the solid. Show your working and simplify your expression.

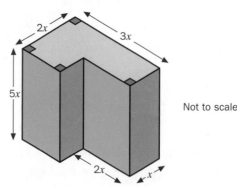

Not to scale

_____

_____

Handling data

Collecting data			Studied	Revised	Assessment questions
8.1	Identifying and selecting data	– Types of data – Bias			
8.2	Collecting data				
8.3	Organising data	– Tables and charts – Two-way tables			

Representing and interpreting data			Studied	Revised	Assessment questions
9.1	Statistical diagrams	– Pictograms – Bar charts – Pie charts – Frequency polygons – Line graphs and time series – Scatter graphs – Misleading graphs			
9.2	Averages and range	– Averages of discrete data – Finding averages from a frequency table – Stem-and-leaf diagrams – Averages of grouped data – Finding the mean from a frequency diagram – Comparing sets of data			
9.3	Cumulative frequency graphs	– Finding the median – Finding and using the interquartile range – Box plots			

Probability			Studied	Revised	Assessment questions
10.1	The probability scale	– Probability of an event happening – Probability of an event not happening			
10.2	Possible outcomes for two successive events	– Lists – Sample-space diagrams – Two-way tables – The addition law – The multiplication law – Tree diagrams			
10.3	Estimating probability	– Relative frequency			

8 Collecting data

Learning Summary

After studying this section you should be able to:

- identify and obtain necessary information to solve a mathematical problem
- identify and select necessary data
- collect and record discrete data
- group data where appropriate into equal class intervals
- design a survey, questionnaire or experiment identifying possible sources of bias

8.1 Identifying and selecting data

> **Key Point**
>
> Every day people are bombarded with information called **data**. Data is often collected to test a hypothesis. (A hypothesis is a theory or explanation that has not been proved.)

Types of data

Discrete data can only take particular values. It is often found by counting. An example is the number of cars in a car park.

Continuous data can take any value in a given range. Such data is often found by measuring. Examples include the height and weight of year 8 pupils.

Primary data is data that you collect yourself.

Secondary data is data that somebody else has collected. For example, a census is carried out every 10 years in order to provide a 'snapshot' of people living in Britain. The census is a very rich source of data that is analysed to help the authorities plan for the future.

Bias

(Level 7) In data handling, the word **population** is used for a set, collection or group of objects that are being studied.

A **sample** is a small part of a population.

If you are collecting information make sure that there is no bias.

Anything that distorts the data in a sample, so that it will not give a representative picture of a population, is called **bias**.

Bias usually occurs in two ways:
- If the population or sample is not correctly chosen.
- Through the style of questioning, for example, if your opinion is evident: 'Most people want a new swimming pool. Do you want a new swimming pool?'

To avoid bias, ask a sample large enough to represent the whole population but small enough to be manageable.

An example of a biased sample would be whilst investigating homework trends at a school to only ask pupils in year 7 how much homework they do. This is biased because no other year groups have been taken into account.

Key Point

When identifying and selecting data, start with enough **primary** or **secondary** data so that a sample can be taken from it. Make sure that the sample is not biased.

For example, Rhysian is carrying out a survey into how often people do a sporting activity. She will need to ask sufficient people; 10 would be too small, so a sample of 50 people would be more reflective. She will need to ask a wide cross-section of people (i.e. a wide range of ages and both males and females).

Where Rhysian does her survey is also important. For example, her survey would be biased if she stood outside a leisure centre because the people she would ask are more likely to do a sporting activity.

Progress Check

1 Which of the following are primary data and which are secondary?
   (a) Finding out information on a holiday destination by looking on the Internet.
   (b) Measuring the height of all the pupils in your class.
   (c) Finding out the shoe size of pupils in your class.
   (d) Looking at records to see how many babies were born in January.
   (e) Looking at tables of the number of road traffic accidents each year.
2 Explain why this sample is biased:
   'Investigating the pattern of absences for a school by studying the registers in February.'

(ii) the pattern of truancy might vary at different times in the year
2. This might be biased because students are: (i) more likely to be ill in the winter months
1. (a) Secondary   (b) Primary   (c) Primary   (d) Secondary   (e) Secondary

8.2 Collecting data

There are some standard ways of collecting data.

By observation

Here an **observation sheet** (sometimes known as a **data collection sheet**) can be used. There are a few points to consider:
- Is the observation sheet clear and easy to use?

- Does the observation sheet actually answer the question asked?
- Was the data collected for long enough?
- Do the time and place of the observation affect the results?

For example, here is an observation sheet used to test the hypothesis: 'Most staff at the school have a red car.'

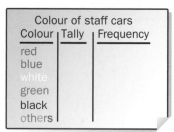

Colour of staff cars		
Colour	Tally	Frequency
red		
blue		
white		
green		
black		
others		

By experiment

Experiments can be carried out in order to collect data. Important points to consider are:
- Does the experiment test the **hypothesis**?
- Have sufficient experiments been carried out to provide enough results to reflect what is happening?

By questionnaires

When designing or using questionnaires, the following points must be considered:
- Ask questions that cover the purpose of the survey.
- Keep the questions simple so that the answers are easy to analyse.
- Do not ask for information that is not needed, e.g. name or age.
- Make sure that your opinion is not evident, e.g. 'Do you agree that 'Coronation Street' is better than 'EastEnders'?'
- Give response boxes for all possible outcomes. They should not overlap.
- Include a time frame if needed.

> When carrying out a survey using a questionnaire, make sure you ask a cross-section of people.

For example:

How much do you spend on magazines each week? ◄── Time frame

Under £1 [ ]   £1–£1.99 [ ]   £2–£2.99 [ ]   £3 or more [ ]

Not overlapping

8.3 Organising data

Tables and charts

Data that has been collected can be sorted by putting it into a table called a **tally chart** or **frequency table**.

Tally charts

A tally chart shows the frequency of each item (how often the item occurs).

A **tally** is a mark I. When the marks are grouped into fives they are easy to count. The fifth mark forms a gate ЖНТ.

For example:

Hair colour	Tally	Frequency
Brown	ЖНТ IIII	9
Ginger	IIII	4
Black	ЖНТ II	7
Blond	ЖНТ ЖНТ II	12

There is one tally mark for each pupil.

Adding the tallies gives the frequency of each hair colour.

Grouped data

If the data covers a large range of results, it is usual to group it into **class intervals**. Usually each class interval is the same width.

For example, in a test out of 50 the scores might be grouped as:
0–10, 11–20, 21–30, 31–40, 41–50.

It is sensible to choose groupings of size 2, 5 or 10. For this example the class intervals are not the same size because the first group has a range of 11 and the others have a range of 10. A frequency table for the test might look like this:

The class intervals must not overlap.

This is **discrete** data. You can score 41 or 42 but not 41.3

Score	Tally	Frequency
0–10	III	3
11–20	ЖНТ II	7
21–30	IIII	4
31–40	ЖНТ ЖНТ	10
41–50	I	1

For **continuous** data, the class intervals are usually written using inequalities.

For example, the table below shows the height in cm of 30 pupils.

Height (cm)	Tally	Frequency
$120 \leqslant h < 130$	ЖНТ I	6
$130 \leqslant h < 140$	ЖНТ	5
$140 \leqslant h < 150$	ЖНТ ЖНТ IIII	14
$150 \leqslant h < 160$	ЖНТ	5

$120 \leqslant h < 130$ means that the heights are between 120 and 130cm.
$120 \leqslant h$ means the height can be equal to 120cm.
$h < 130$ means the height cannot be equal to 130cm. 130cm would be in the next class interval.

Two-way tables

Two-way tables are used to show two sets of information about the same group of individuals.

For example, a teacher has conducted a survey of the students in year 8 to find out their favourite subject:

	Maths	English	Science	Total
Boys	20	10	15	45
Girls	30	20	10	60
Total	50	30	25	105

The table shows that 20 boys preferred Maths and 30 students preferred English.

Progress Check

1. Design a data collection sheet that could be used to investigate the hypothesis: 'Most people prefer watching comedies on the TV.'
2. 100 pupils went on a day trip during activities week. Copy and complete the table.

	Swimming	Theme park	Zoo	Total
Boys	7	20		30
Girls	35			
Total	42		15	100

2.

	Swimming	Theme park	Zoo	Total
Boys	7	20	3	30
Girls	35	23	12	70
Total	42	43	15	100

1.

Type of TV programme	Tally	Frequency
Comedy		
Soap		
Drama		
Thriller		
Others		

Assessment questions

Try the following questions.

Level 4 **1.** Ahmed and Lucy are collecting information on the type of television programmes their friends watch. Draw a suitable data collection sheet that they could use.

Level 4 **2.** After completing their survey, Ahmed and Lucy obtained the following results:

C = comedy   C   C   F   S   S   S   F
S = soap   C   C   S   C   S   C   F
F = film   F   S   F   S   C   C   C

Represent this information in a tally chart.

Level 5 **3.** A group of year 9 students took part in a mental arithmetic test. The marks they scored are shown below.

12	9	41	34	21	17	6	15	50	47
15	37	36	41	27	24	20	17	39	32
6	42	19	37	41	48	50	26	48	30

(a) Using class intervals 1–10, 11–20, 21–30, 31–40 and 41–50, construct a frequency table.

(b) Which class interval has the highest frequency? _____

Level 6 **4.** You are asked to do a survey outside a sports centre to find out about its popularity.

(a) One of the questions is: 'How old are you?'

Under 10 [ ]   10–20 [ ]   20–30 [ ]   30–40 [ ]   Over 40 [ ]

Explain what is wrong with this question.

_____

(b) Another question is:

'Do you go swimming?'   Sometimes [ ]   Occasionally [ ]   Often [ ]

Explain what is wrong with this question.

_____

Level 7 **5.** A market research company interviewed people travelling by car and by train.
45 out of the 100 car travellers had travelled 20 miles or less.
Of the 250 people interviewed, 85 had travelled more than 20 miles.
Use a two-way table to find out the number of people who had travelled more than 20 miles by train.

_____

Level 7 **6.** Audrey and Colin are carrying out a survey to find out if people are going to use a new supermarket. Listed below are some of the ways they might collect their data.
For each method, decide whether or not their sample will be biased.

(a) Asking all the households in the road where the supermarket is situated. _____

(b) Conducting a telephone survey of a randomly-chosen set of households from the telephone book. _____

(c) Conducting a survey at the train station by asking every tenth person. _____

(d) Asking a group of 10–18 year olds at the local school. _____

9 Representing and interpreting data

Learning Summary

After studying this section you should be able to:

- select and represent data using a variety of statistical diagrams
- identify which statistical diagram is most useful for a problem
- interpret statistical diagrams
- find and interpret averages of different data to compare distributions
- estimate and find the median and interquartile range for large data sets
- draw and interpret cumulative frequency diagrams

9.1 Statistical diagrams

Data can be shown in several different types of diagram.

Pictograms

Pictograms use symbols: each symbol represents a certain number of items.

Make sure when drawing pictograms that:

- each row is labelled
- each symbol is the same size, with equal gaps between them
- a key is given.

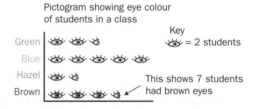

Pictogram showing eye colour of students in a class

Key

👁 = 2 students

Green

Blue

Hazel

Brown — This shows 7 students had brown eyes

Bar charts

A **bar chart** is a set of bars or columns of **equal** width. Bar charts are drawn with gaps between the bars. The height of each bar shows the frequency. Bar charts are used for discrete data. Dual and compound bar charts can be used to compare data.

Frequency is always on the vertical axis.

For example:

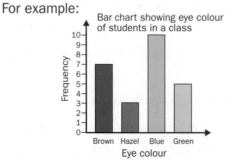

Bar chart showing eye colour of students in a class

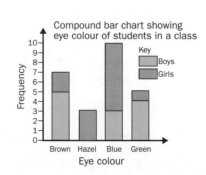

Compound bar chart showing eye colour of students in a class

Key
Boys
Girls

Sometimes lines are used instead of bars:

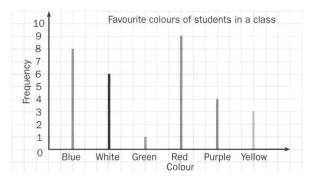

> This is known as a **bar line** graph.

If the data is continuous, the bars must touch. This is a **frequency diagram** or **histogram**.

> The data must be grouped into equal **class intervals** if the length of the bar is used to represent the frequency.

For example, the masses of 30 workers in a factory are shown in the table.

Mass (M kg)	Frequency
$45 < M \leqslant 55$	7
$55 < M \leqslant 65$	13
$65 < M \leqslant 75$	6
$75 < M \leqslant 85$	4
Total	30

Remember the following:
- The axes do not need to start at zero. Attention is usually drawn to this fact by using a jagged line like this $\lessgtr$.
- The axes are labelled and the graph has a title.

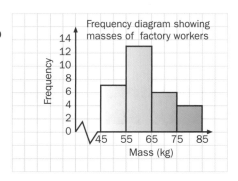

The diagram shows that the largest group of workers has a mass between 55 and 65kg.

Pie charts

In a pie chart the data is shown in a circle, which is split up into sections. Each section represents a certain number of items.

Drawing pie charts

When calculating the angles for a pie chart:
- find the total of the items listed
- find the fraction of the total for each item
- multiply the fraction by 360° to find the angle.

> It is useful to know how to construct statistical diagrams on a computer.

For example, the table opposite gives the hair colour of 24 ten-year-olds.

Hair colour	Frequency
Brown	8
Auburn	4
Blond	6
Black	6
Total	24

8 out of 24 have brown hair so $\frac{8}{24} \times 360° = 120°$

Key in on the calculator

$\boxed{8} \div \boxed{24} \times \boxed{360} \boxed{=}$

Auburn: $\frac{4}{24} \times 360° = 60°$

Blond: $\frac{6}{24} \times 360° = 90°$

Black: $\frac{6}{24} \times 360° = 90°$

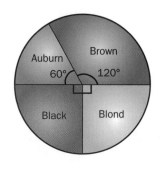

Interpreting pie charts

Sometimes you will be given a pie chart and asked to work out the numbers it represents.

Example

The pie chart shows how some students spent Saturday night. If 140 pupils went to the ice rink, how many went to the disco and the cinema?

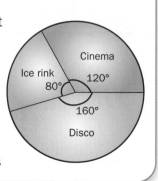

80° represents 140 pupils
1° represents $\frac{140}{80}$ = 1.75 pupils
Number at disco = 160° × 1.75 = 280 pupils
Number at cinema = 120° × 1.75 = 210 pupils

Frequency polygons

(Level 7) To draw a **frequency polygon**, join the midpoints at the top of each bar in the frequency diagram.

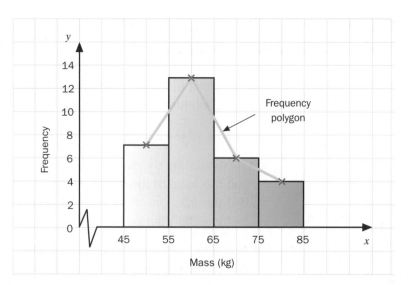

Key Point

Frequency polygons can be superimposed on top of each other to compare results.

For example, these two frequency polygons show the distances jumped in a high-jump competition by pupils in year 7 and year 9.

From the polygons we can see that in general a greater proportion of pupils from year 9 jumped greater heights.

It is important that you can interpret diagrams like these.

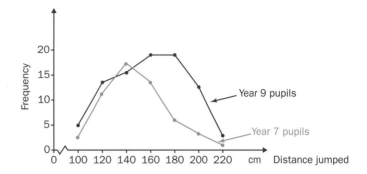

Line graphs and time series

Line graphs are a set of points joined by lines. Line graphs can be used to show continuous data, and show how a quantity changes over time.

For example:

Year	2000	2001	2002	2003	2004	2005	2006	2007
Number of cars sold	420	530	480	560	590	620	490	440

The middle values (for example at Y) have no meaning. Point Y does not mean that halfway between 2005 and 2006, 550 cars were sold.

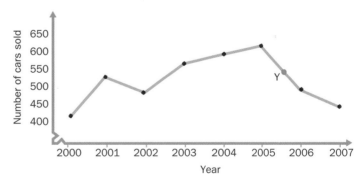

A **time series** is made up of numerical data recorded at intervals of time and plotted as a line graph.

The diagram below shows a time series showing seasonal fluctuations.

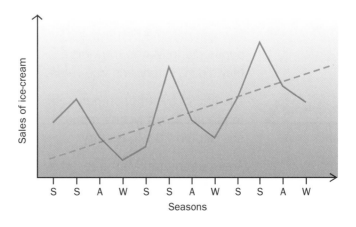

Scatter graphs

Key Point

A **scatter graph** (**scatter diagram** or **scatter plot**) can be used to show if two sets of data are related. Its importance is to show the **correlation** (connection) between the data.

Correlation

Correlation is a measurement of how strong the relationship is between two sets of data. There are three types of correlation:

Positive correlation	Negative correlation	Zero or no correlation
Both variables are increasing. If the points are nearly on a straight line there is said to be a **strong positive correlation**.	One variable increases whilst the other decreases. In the graph above there is a **strong negative correlation**.	There is no linear correlation between the variables.

The line of best fit

Key Point

(Level 7) The line of best fit is the **line** that **best fits** the data. The line goes in the direction of the data and has roughly the same number of points above it as below it. A line of best fit can be used to make predictions.

For example, the table below shows the Maths and History results of 11 pupils.

Maths test (%)	64	79	38	42	49	75	83	82	66	61	54
History test (%)	70	36	84	70	74	42	29	33	50	56	64

The data is plotted on a scatter graph, which suggests that there is a **strong negative correlation** – in general, the better the pupils did in Maths the worse they did in History, and vice versa.

The line of best fit can be used to predict Amy's Maths result if she scored 78% in History.

Amy's estimated Maths result is approximately 43%.

> Draw lines across and up the graph to help.

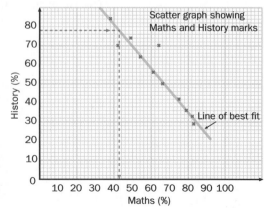

Scatter graph showing Maths and History marks

Misleading graphs

Statistical graphs are sometimes misleading: they do not always tell the true story. Here are some examples:

This graph is misleading because it has no scales and the bars are not the same width.

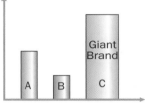

> Watch out for graphs that do not have a vertical scale starting at zero. They are commonly seen when a product is being advertised.

This graph is misleading because the scales do not start at zero, hence the differences between the bars look much bigger than they actually are.

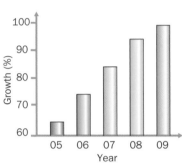

This pictogram is misleading because the pictures change size. Although Brand B has only sold twice the amount of Brand A, it gives the impression of having sold much more.

Brand A
10 000 sold

Brand B
20 000 sold

Progress Check

1. The pie chart shows the favourite subjects of 720 girls. 🖩
   (a) How many girls like Maths?
   (b) How many girls like Art?

Maths 140°
Art 70°
30° RS
120° PE

2. (Level 7) **(a)** What type of correlation does the scatter graph show?
   (b) Draw on the line of best fit.

3. Explain why this graph is misleading.

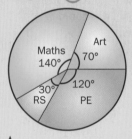

3. There are no scales and bar B is wider than bar A.

2. (a) Positive correlation – the better you did in Test 1, the better you did in Test 2. (b) The line of best fit should follow the direction of the data and have roughly the same number of points above it as below it.

1. (a) 280 girls   (b) 140 girls

9.2 Averages and range

Averages of discrete data

Key Point	You should know three types of average: **mean**, **median** and **mode**. The **range** tells us the **spread** of the data.

Mean – sometimes known as the 'average'

$$\text{Mean} = \frac{\text{sum of a set of values}}{\text{the number of values used}}$$

Median – the middle value when the data is put in order of size

Mode – the value that occurs the most often

Range – highest value minus the lowest value

For example, a football team scored the following number of goals in their first ten matches:

2, 4, 0, 1, 2, 2, 3, 6, 2, 4

Mean $= \dfrac{2 + 4 + 0 + 1 + 2 + 2 + 3 + 6 + 2 + 4}{10} = \dfrac{26}{10} = 2.6$ goals

Median = 0, 1, 2, 2, 2, 2, 3, 4, 4, 6 ← Put in order of size first.

> If there are two numbers in the middle, the median is halfway between them.

$= \cancel{0}, \cancel{1}, 2, 2, 2, 2, \cancel{3}, \cancel{4}, \cancel{4}, \cancel{6}$

$\dfrac{2 + 2}{2} = 2$ goals

Mode = 2 goals

Range = 6 – 0 = 6

Example

The mean of four numbers is 20; the mean of six other numbers is 36. What is the mean of all ten numbers?

The sum of the four numbers is $4 \times 20 = 80 \left(\dfrac{80}{4} = 20\right)$

The sum of the six numbers is $6 \times 36 = 216 \left(\dfrac{216}{6} = 36\right)$

Mean of all ten numbers is $\dfrac{80 + 216}{10} = \dfrac{296}{10} = 29.6$

The mean is useful when a typical value is wanted. It should not really be used if there are extreme values, e.g. for data such as 1, 2, 3, 4, 65.
The median is a useful average when there are extreme values.
The mode is useful when the most common value is needed.

Finding averages from a frequency table

A frequency table tells us how many items are in a group.

Example

The table shows the number of sisters of children in a year 7 class. Find the mean, median, mode and range.

Number of sisters (x)	0	1	2	3	4	5
Frequency	4	9	3	5	2	0

> Remember to divide by the sum of the frequency.

$$\text{Mean} = \frac{\text{total of the results of frequency} \times \text{number of sisters}}{\text{total of the frequency}}$$

$$= \frac{(4 \times 0) + (9 \times 1) + (3 \times 2) + (5 \times 3) + (2 \times 4) + (0 \times 5)}{4 + 9 + 3 + 5 + 2 + 0}$$

$$= \frac{38}{23} = 1.65 \text{ (2 d.p.)}$$

Median
There are 23 people altogether; the middle person is the 12th one. Looking at the table, the 12th person has 1 sister.

Mode
This is the number of sisters with the highest frequency, that is 1 sister.

Range
4 – 0 = 4 sisters

Stem-and-leaf diagrams

Stem-and-leaf diagrams are another way of recording information and they can be used to find the mode, median and range of a set of data.

Example

Here are some marks gained by some students in a Maths examination.

24 61 55 36 42
32 60 51 38 58
55 52 47 55 55

Example (cont.)

Put the information into a stem-and-leaf diagram.

Stem is 30,
leaf is 2,
i.e. 32

Stem	Leaf
2	4
3	2 6 8
4	7 2
5	5 2 5 1 5 5 8
6	1 0

Key = 2 | 4 means 24

Rewriting in order gives

2	4
3	②6 8
4	2 7
5	1 2 5 5 5 5 8
6	0 1

Key = 2 | 4 means 24

To read off the values, you multiply the stem by 10 and add on the leaf.

Using the stem-and-leaf diagram the mode, median and range can be found.

Mode = 55

Median is at the eighth score, i.e. 52

Range = 61 − 24 = 37

Averages of grouped data

Key Point

(Level 7) When the data is grouped, the exact values are not known. An **estimate** of the **mean** can be calculated by using the **midpoint** of the class interval. (The midpoint is the halfway value.)

For example, the heights of some year 9 pupils are shown in the table below.

Height (h cm)	Frequency (f)	Midpoint (x)	$f \times x$
$140 \leqslant h < 145$	4	142.5	570
$145 \leqslant h < 150$	7	147.5	1032.5
$150 \leqslant h < 155$	14	152.5	2135
$155 \leqslant h < 160$	5	157.5	787.5
$160 \leqslant h < 165$	2	162.5	325

Σ is the Greek letter sigma and means 'sum of'. $\bar{x}$ stands for the mean.

Mean $(\bar{x}) = \dfrac{\Sigma fx}{\Sigma f}$

$= \dfrac{(142.5 \times 4) + (147.5 \times 7) + (152.5 \times 14) + (157.5 \times 5) + (162.5 \times 2)}{4 + 7 + 14 + 5 + 2}$

$= \dfrac{4850}{32}$

$= 151.6$cm (1 d.p.)

Modal class

Because the data is grouped, the modal class is used instead of the mode. Here the modal class is $150 \leqslant h < 155$ as it is the class interval with the highest frequency.

Median

For grouped data, we can find the class interval containing the median. There are 32 people in the survey; the middle person is between the 16th and 17th persons. Both have heights in the class interval $150 \leqslant h < 155$. So, the class interval containing the median is $150 \leqslant h < 155$.

Finding the mean from a frequency diagram

(Level 7) Sometimes you might be asked to estimate the mean from a frequency diagram.

> Remember to use the midpoint multiplied by the frequency.

Example

The frequency diagram shows some students' heights. Estimate the mean height.

First work out the midpoints and frequency of each bar.

$\Sigma fx = (122.5 \times 2) + (127.5 \times 4)$
$\quad + (132.5 \times 1) + (137.5 \times 8)$
$\quad + (142.5 \times 7) + (147.5 \times 4)$
$\quad + (152.5 \times 4)$

$\dfrac{\Sigma fx}{\Sigma f} = \dfrac{4185}{30}$ Mean height = 139.5cm

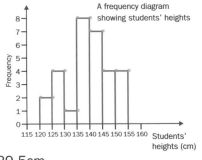

A frequency diagram showing students' heights

Comparing sets of data

The range and averages are used to compare sets of data.

For example, 8M obtained a mean of 57% in a test. The top mark was 100% and the bottom mark 21%. 8T obtained a mean of 84% in the test. The top mark was 94% and the bottom mark 76%.

From the averages, 8T performed better than 8M.
Now look at the range for each class:
8M = 100% − 21% = 79%   8T = 94% − 76% = 18%

The range shows that 8M's marks were much more widely spread than 8T's. Some pupils in 8M obtained higher marks than some in 8T.

Progress Check

1. The heights in cm of some students are:
   154, 172, 160, 164, 168, 177, 181, 140, 142, 153, 154, 153, 162
   (a) Draw a stem-and-leaf diagram for this information.
   (b) What is the range?
   (c) What is the median?
2. (Level 7) The length of the roots of some plants is recorded in the table opposite.
   (a) Find an estimate for the mean length. 🖩
   (b) What is the modal class?

Length l (cm)	Frequency	Midpoint (x)
$0 \leqslant l < 5$	6	2.5
$5 \leqslant l < 10$	9	
$10 \leqslant l < 15$	15	
$15 \leqslant l < 20$	9	
$20 \leqslant l < 25$	6	
$25 \leqslant l < 30$	2	

2. (a) Mean: 13.1cm (3 s.f.)   (b) Modal class $10 \leqslant l < 15$
Key: 14 | 0 means 140cm
18 | 1
17 | 2 7
16 | 0 2 4 8
15 | 3 3 4 4
14 | 0 2
(c) Median = 160cm
(b) Range = 41cm
1. (a)

135

9.3 Cumulative frequency graphs

(Level 8) Cumulative frequency graphs are very useful for finding the median and the spread of grouped data. Before drawing the graph, the **cumulative frequencies** have to be obtained by adding together the frequencies to give a **running total**.

For example, the table shows the time in minutes for 49 pupils' journey times to school.

> The frequencies are added together to get the cumulative frequencies.

Time (t minutes)	Frequency	Time (t minutes)	Cumulative frequency
$0 \leqslant t < 10$	15	$0 \leqslant t < 10$	15
$10 \leqslant t < 20$	16	$0 \leqslant t < 20$	31 (15 + 16)
$20 \leqslant t < 30$	9	$0 \leqslant t < 30$	40 (31 + 9)
$30 \leqslant t < 40$	6	$0 \leqslant t < 40$	46 (40 + 6)
$40 \leqslant t < 50$	3	$0 \leqslant t < 50$	49 (46 + 3)

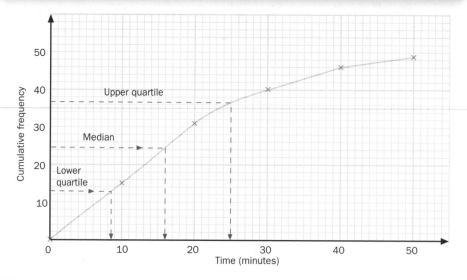

When drawing the graph, follow these steps:
- When plotting the points, the **upper class limits** must be plotted. Plot (10, 15), (20, 31), (30, 40), etc.
- Since no one took less than zero time, the graph starts at (0, 0).
- Join the points with a smooth curve.

Finding the median

The cumulative frequency curve can be used to estimate the median. The median is the middle value of the distribution.

For the journey time data:
Median = $\frac{1}{2}$ × total cumulative frequency = $\frac{1}{2}$ × 49 = 24.5

Find 24.5 on the vertical scale and read across to the curve and then down. This shows the median = 16 minutes.

Finding and using the interquartile range

The interquartile range = upper quartile – lower quartile

Upper quartile – this is the value three-quarters of the way into the distribution. For the data on page 136, that is $\frac{3}{4} \times 49 = 36.75$ th value.

Lower quartile – this is the value one-quarter of the way into the distribution. For the data on page 136, that is $\frac{1}{4} \times 49 = 12.25$ th value.

As before, read across at the appropriate places on the vertical scale.
Upper quartile = 25   Lower quartile = 8.5

Interquartile range = 25 – 8.5 = 16.5
A large interquartile range indicates that the data is widely spread. A small interquartile range indicates that the data is concentrated about the median.

Box plots

A box plot shows the interquartile range as a box, which makes it useful when comparing distributions. The following box plot shows the journey times on page 136.

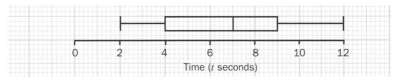

Example

The times in seconds taken by 11 students to solve a puzzle are listed in order: 2   4   4   5   5   7   8   8   9   11   12

Lower quartile   Median   Upper quartile

Draw a box plot of this data. 2, 4, 4, 5, 5, 7, 8, 8, 9, 11, 12

Progress Check

Josie carried out a survey for her geography coursework. She recorded the distance travelled to an out-of-town shopping centre. Her results are shown in the table.

1. Draw a cumulative frequency graph.
2. Work out:
   (a) the median
   (b) the interquartile range for this data.

Distance (d miles)	Frequency
$0 \leqslant d < 5$	15
$5 \leqslant d < 10$	60
$10 \leqslant d < 15$	67
$15 \leqslant d < 20$	30
$20 \leqslant d < 25$	22
$25 \leqslant d < 30$	6

2. (a) Median = 12 miles (approx.)   (b) Interquartile range = 9 miles (approx.)
1. A cumulative frequency graph should be plotted with the points
(0, 0), (5, 15), (10, 75), (15, 142), (20, 172), (25, 194), (30, 200).

Assessment questions

Try the following questions.

Level 4 **1.** Here is a dual bar chart showing the number of hours of TV that Emma and William watched last week.

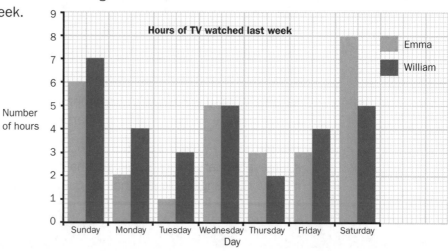

(a) Write down the number of hours of TV that Emma watched on Sunday. _____

(b) On which day did Emma and William watch the same number of hours of TV?

_____

(c) Work out the total number of hours of TV that William watched on Sunday and Monday.

_____

(d) Who watched the greater number of hours of TV on Friday and Saturday? Show your working.

_____

Level 5 **2.** The graph shows the temperature outside every day at midday on one week in July.

(a) How hot was it at midday on Wednesday?

_____

(b) On which day was it the hottest at midday?

_____

(c) Which two days had the same temperature at midday?

_____

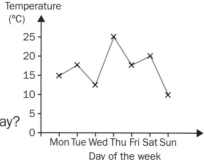

Level 5 **3.** Rajesh was playing a game. His scores were: 12, 36, 14, 9, 3, 5

Work out: 🖩

(a) the mean _____

(b) the median _____

(c) the range. _____

Level 5 **4.** Diana has six cards:

The six cards have a mean of 8 and a range of 8. What must the two other cards be?

_____   _____

138

Assessment questions

Level 6 **5.** A census of two towns was carried out to look at the proportions of age within each town. The pie charts show the results.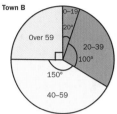

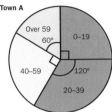

Town A has 3750 0–19 year olds.   Town B has 1500 40–59 year olds.

(a) How many 20–39 year olds live in Town A? _____

(b) How many over 59 year olds live in Town A? _____

(c) How many 20–39 year olds live in Town B? _____

(d) Archie says, 'There are more over 59 year olds living in Town B because the angle of the pie chart is bigger.' Is Archie correct? Give a reason for your answer.

_____

(e) A new school will be built. In which town should the school be built and why?

_____

Level 6 **6.** Look at the scatter graphs.

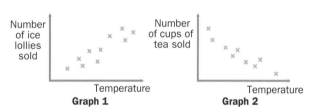

Graph 1   Graph 2

(a) What does graph 1 tell you about the relationship between the number of ice lollies sold and the temperature?

_____

(b) What does graph 2 tell you about the relationship between the number of cups of tea sold and the temperature?

_____

Level 7 **7.** The height of some seedlings is displayed in the table.

(a) Draw a frequency polygon of this information.

(b) Write down the modal class. _____

(c) Calculate an estimate of the mean height of the seedlings.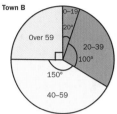

_____

Height (h cm)	Number
$0 \leqslant h < 5$	4
$5 \leqslant h < 10$	7
$10 \leqslant h < 15$	10
$15 \leqslant h < 20$	3
$20 \leqslant h < 25$	2

Level 8 **8.** The length of the roots of some plants is shown in the table.

(a) Draw a cumulative frequency graph. Use scales of 1cm to 10cm on the cumulative frequency axis and 1cm to 5cm on the length axis.

(b) Find the median length. _____

(c) Find the interquartile range. _____

(d) Draw a box plot for the data.

Length (l cm)	Frequency
$0 \leqslant l < 5$	6
$5 \leqslant l < 10$	9
$10 \leqslant l < 15$	15
$15 \leqslant l < 20$	9
$20 \leqslant l < 25$	6
$25 \leqslant l < 30$	2

10 Probability

Learning Summary

After studying this section you should be able to:

- understand and use the probability scale from 0 to 1
- find the theoretical probability of an event
- calculate the probability of an event not happening
- find and record all mutually exclusive outcomes for single events and two successive events in a systematic way
- know when to add and multiply two probabilities
- draw and use tree diagrams
- understand relative frequency as an estimate of probability

10.1 The probability scale

Key Point

Probability is the chance of something happening. All probabilities lie between 0 and 1 and can be written as fractions, decimals or percentages.

Probabilities can be shown on a probability scale. The scale starts at 0 for something that is **impossible** and finishes at 1 for something that is **certain** to happen.

For example:

If you are answering questions on probability, always check that your answer is not greater than 1. If it is, it must be incorrect.

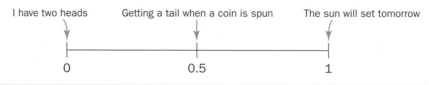

Example

A bag contains 3 red, 6 green and 3 blue beads.
If a bead is chosen at random:
(a) mark with a P the probability of choosing a green bead
(b) mark with a T the probability of choosing a red bead
(c) mark with an X the probability of choosing a black bead.

P is at 0.5 – it has an evens chance of being chosen since half of the beads are green.

X is at 0 since there are no black beads – so a black bead will definitely not be chosen.

T is only a quarter of the way along the scale because only $\frac{1}{4}$ of the beads are red.

Exhaustive events account for all the possible outcomes. For example 1, 2, 3, 4, 5, 6 are all the possible outcomes when a fair dice is thrown.

Probability of an event happening

Key Point

If we know what all the possible outcomes are, we can calculate the probability of something happening:

Probability of an event = $\dfrac{\text{number of ways an event can happen}}{\text{total number of outcomes}}$

P(event) is the shortened way of writing the probability of an event.

Examples

(a) The letters in the word MATHEMATICS are placed in a container, and a letter is taken out at random. What is the probability of taking out:

(i) a letter T?
$P(T) = \frac{2}{11}$

(ii) a letter S?
$P(S) = \frac{1}{11}$

> Since there are 11 letters, each of the probabilities are out of 11.

(iii) a letter R?
$P(R) = 0$

> Since there is no letter R, the probability is zero.

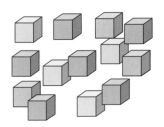

> Remember to write 0 not $\frac{0}{11}$.

(b) Thomas has some coloured blocks, 3 red, 4 blue and 6 green, in a large bag. If he picks out a block at random, what is the probability that the block is:

(i) red?
$P(red) = \frac{3}{13}$

(ii) blue?
$P(blue) = \frac{4}{13}$

(iii) blue, green or red?
$P(blue, green\ or\ red) = \frac{13}{13} = 1$

(iv) white?
$P(white) = 0$

> All the probabilities add up to 1, since Thomas will definitely choose a red, blue or green-coloured block.

Probability of an event not happening

Mutually exclusive events are those events that cannot happen at the same time, for example getting a 6 and a 1 on one throw of a dice.

Key Point

For mutually exclusive events, since the sum of the probabilities is 1, then P(event will not happen) = 1 − P(event will happen).

Examples

(a) The probability that it will rain tomorrow is $\frac{2}{9}$.
What is the probability that it will not rain tomorrow?

P(will not rain) = 1 − P(it will rain)
P(will not rain) = 1 − $\frac{2}{9}$
$\qquad\qquad\quad$ = $\frac{7}{9}$

(b) Some discs are placed in a bag. Most are marked with the number 1, 2, 3, 4 or 5. The rest are unmarked. The probability of picking out a disc marked with a particular number is:

P(1) = 0.2
P(2) = 0.1
P(3) = 0.05
P(4) = 0.15
P(5) = 0.35

What is the probability of picking a disc:
(i) marked with 2, 3 or 4?

$\qquad$ P(2, 3 or 4) = (0.1 + 0.05 + 0.15)
$\qquad\qquad\qquad$ = 0.3

(ii) not marked with a number?

$\qquad$ P(not marked with a number) = 1 − P(marked with a number)
$\qquad\qquad\qquad\qquad\qquad\qquad$ = 1 − (0.2 + 0.1 + 0.05 + 0.15 + 0.35)
$\qquad\qquad\qquad\qquad\qquad\qquad$ = 1 − 0.85
$\qquad\qquad\qquad\qquad\qquad\qquad$ = 0.15

Progress Check

① Use one of these words or phrases to complete each statement.
impossible   very unlikely   unlikely   evens   likely   certain
(a) It is ... that 15 people in the same class have the same birthday.
(b) It is ... that the prime minister will have two heads tomorrow.
(c) It is ... that most people will wear a coat when it is raining.

② A bag contains 6 red and 5 blue counters. If a counter is chosen at random from the bag, find the probability that the counter is:
(a) red
(b) blue
(c) red or blue
(d) yellow

③ The probability that a torch works is 0.63
What is the probability that the torch will not work?

3. 0.37
2. (a) $\frac{6}{11}$ (b) $\frac{5}{11}$ (c) $\frac{11}{11}$ = 1 (d) 0
1. (a) very unlikely (b) impossible (c) likely

10.2 Possible outcomes for two successive events

Lists, tree diagrams and tables are useful when answering probability questions with two successive events.

Lists

Making lists of possible outcomes of two events are useful but only when the items are written in an ordered way.

Examples

(a) A coin can land in two ways: head up (H) or tail up (T). If the coin is tossed twice, make a list of the four possible ways that the coin can land in two throws. What is the probability of getting two heads?

H   H
T   T
H   T
T   H

$P(2H) = \frac{1}{4}$

(b) For her lunch Lin can choose a main course and a dessert from the options shown opposite. List all the possible outcomes of her lunch. What is the probability that Lin will choose pizza and cake?

Pizza, yoghurt   Chicken pie, yoghurt   Fish, yoghurt
Pizza, cake   Chicken pie, cake   Fish, cake

$P(\text{pizza, cake}) = \frac{1}{6}$

Sample-space diagrams

Example

The hands on these two spinners are spun at the same time.

The two scores are added together.
(a) Represent the outcomes on a sample-space diagram.
(b) What is the probability of a score of 7?
    The probability of a score of $7 = \frac{3}{16}$
(c) What is the probability of a multiple of 3?
    The probability of a multiple of $3 = \frac{5}{16}$

There are 16 possible outcomes.

		Spinner 2		
	1	2	2	3
2	3	4	4	5
3	4	5	5	6
4	5	6	6	7
5	6	7	7	8

Spinner 1

It is important to keep a check on the outcomes that you have used. Using a circle or square helps to do that.

Two-way tables

> ### Example
>
> The two-way table shows the number of students in a class who are left-handed or right-handed.
>
> | Hand | Male | Female | Total |
> |------|------|--------|-------|
> | Right | 14 | 10 | 24 |
> | Left | 2 | 7 | 9 |
> | Total | 16 | 17 | 33 |
>
> **(a)** What is the probability that a person chosen at random is right-handed?
>
> P(right-handed) = $\frac{24}{33}$
>
> **(b)** If a boy is chosen at random, what is the probability that he is left-handed?
>
> P(left-handed) = $\frac{2}{16} = \frac{1}{8}$ ← 2 out of the 16 boys are left-handed.

The addition law

If two events, A and B, are **mutually exclusive**, the probability of A or B happening is found by adding the probabilities:

P(A or B) = P(A) + P(B)

> ### Example
>
> There are 20 counters in a bag. 6 are red, 5 are white and the rest are blue. Find the probability that if Gill picks a counter at random, it is either red or white.
>
> P(red) = $\frac{6}{20}$ P(white) = $\frac{5}{20}$
>
> P(red or white) = P(red) + P(white)
>
> $\qquad\qquad = \frac{6}{20} + \frac{5}{20}$
>
> $\qquad\qquad = \frac{11}{20}$ ← Red and white are mutually exclusive.
>
>

The multiplication law

Two events are said to be **independent** when the outcome of the second event is not affected by the outcome of the first.

If two or more events are **independent**, the probability of A and B happening together is found by **multiplying** the separate probabilities:

P(A and B) = P(A) × P(B)

Example

The probability that it will be windy on any day in April is $\frac{3}{10}$. Find the probability that it will be:

(a) windy on both April 1st and April 3rd.

P(windy and windy) = $\frac{3}{10} \times \frac{3}{10} = \frac{9}{100}$

(b) windy on April 5th but not on April 20th.

P(windy and not windy) = $\frac{3}{10} \times \frac{7}{10} = \frac{21}{100}$

Tree diagrams

Key Point

Probabilities are written on the branches of the tree diagram and **multiplied** along the branches to obtain the probability of two events happening.

Example

The probability that Charlotte is late for registration is 0.2
(a) Find the probability that Charlotte is late on two successive days.

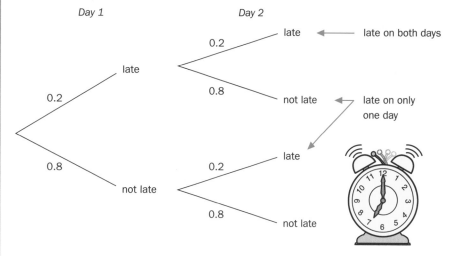

Probability Charlotte is late on both days is 0.2 × 0.2 = 0.04

(b) Find the probability that Charlotte is late on one day only.

(0.2 × 0.8) + (0.8 × 0.2)
= 0.16 + 0.16
= 0.32

If your tree diagram is correct, the probabilities of each pair of branches should add up to 1.

Key Point

Where there is more than one way in which the desired outcome can happen, the **probabilities** for each way are **added** together to find the total probability.

Progress Check

1. Reece has a pizza for his lunch. He has a choice of three toppings: mushroom, pineapple or ham. He chooses two toppings. Make a list of all the possible pizzas he can have.

2. Two fair dice are thrown at the same time and their scores are multiplied. Draw a sample-space diagram to show this information. Work out the probability of:
   (a) a score of 3
   (b) a score that is a multiple of 5.

3. The probability that Ashock does his homework is 0.8
   The probability that David does his homework is 0.45
   Find the probability that both boys do their homework. 🖩

4. The two-way table shows the number of infants who were immunised against an infectious disease and the number of infants who caught the disease.

	Immunised	Not immunised	Total
Did not catch disease	83	8	91
Caught the disease	4	17	21
Total	87	25	112

(a) What is the probability that an infant who has been immunised catches the disease?

(b) What is the probability that an infant has been immunised?

Answers:

1. Mushroom and pineapple, pineapple and ham, mushroom and ham

2.

	Dice 1					
	1	2	3	4	5	6
Dice 2 1	1	2	3	4	5	6
2	2	4	6	8	10	12
3	3	6	9	12	15	18
4	4	8	12	16	20	24
5	5	10	15	20	25	30
6	6	12	18	24	30	36

(a) $\frac{2}{36} = \frac{1}{18}$ (b) $\frac{11}{36}$

3. 0.36

4. (a) $\frac{4}{87}$ (b) $\frac{87}{112}$

10.3 Estimating probability

You can estimate the probabilities of some events by doing an experiment.

The experiment must be repeated several times and a record kept of:
- the number of successful trials (when the event happens)
- the total number of trials.

Key Point

The **estimated probability** of an event $= \dfrac{\text{number of successful trials}}{\text{total number of trials}}$

For example:

Toss a fair coin 100 times. Record your results in a tally chart.

Top side of coin	Tally	Frequency
Head	JHT JHT JHT JHT JHT JHT JHT JHT JHT III	48
Tail	JHT JHT JHT JHT JHT JHT JHT JHT JHT JHT II	52

Using the results, the estimated probability of throwing a head

$$= \frac{\text{number of successful trials}}{\text{total number of trials}}$$

$$= \frac{\text{number of heads}}{\text{total number of tosses}}$$

$$= \frac{48}{100}$$

$$= 0.48$$

This is the estimated probability that the result will be a head.

> The more times the experiment is carried out, the closer the estimated probability gets to the theoretical one.

The probability of some events can be predicted, e.g. the probability of scoring 2 on a fair dice is $\frac{1}{6}$ because all the outcomes (1, 2, 3, 4, 5, 6) are equally likely. A predicted, or theoretical, probability can be used to estimate the expected number of successes in an experiment.

Examples

(a) If a fair dice is thrown 300 times, approximately how many fives are likely to be obtained?

$P(5) = \frac{1}{6} \times 300$ ← Since a 5 is expected $\frac{1}{6}$ of the time.
$P(5) = 50$

You would expect to get 50 fives.

(b) The probability of obtaining a 'C' grade in French at GCSE is 0.4. If 200 students sit the exam, how many are expected to achieve a 'C' grade?

$P(C) = 0.4 \times 200$
$\quad\quad = 80$

Hence, 80 students are expected to achieve a 'C' grade.

Relative frequency

Some probabilities cannot be predicted, e.g. the probability that a piece of toast will land butter-side up. In this case we can repeat an experiment many times and find the **relative frequency** of the toast landing butter-side up.

If the toast lands butter-side up x times in n experiments, the relative frequency of the toast landing butter-side up is $\frac{x}{n}$.

Relative frequency of an event = $\dfrac{\text{number of successful trials}}{\text{total number of trials}}$

The relative frequency of an event is used when you cannot calculate probabilities based on equally likely outcomes.

Surveys allow you to estimate the results of a large group of people by finding the relative frequency with a smaller group.

For example, if a dice is thrown 180 times, it would be expected that about 30 twos would be thrown.

$\frac{1}{6} \times 180 = 30$

If we threw the dice 180 times and recorded the frequency of twos every 30 times, the results may look like:

Number of throws	Total frequency of twos	Relative frequency
30	3	$\left(\frac{3}{30}\right)$ 0.1
60	7	$\left(\frac{7}{60}\right)$ 0.12
90	16	$\left(\frac{16}{90}\right)$ 0.18
120	19	$\left(\frac{19}{120}\right)$ 0.16
150	24	$\left(\frac{24}{150}\right)$ 0.16
180	31	$\left(\frac{31}{180}\right)$ 0.17

Drawing a graph of the results shows that as the number of throws increases, the relative frequency gets closer to the expected probability.

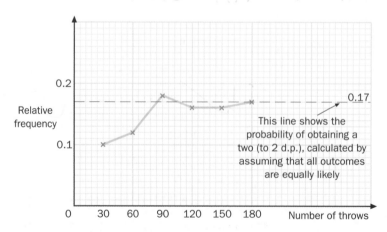

This line shows the probability of obtaining a two (to 2 d.p.), calculated by assuming that all outcomes are equally likely

1. The probability of passing a driving test at the first attempt is 0.65. If there are 200 people taking the test for the first time, how many do you expect to pass the test?
2. When a dice was thrown 320 times, a four came up 58 times. What is the relative frequency of getting a four?
3. The probability of getting flu this winter is $\frac{4}{9}$. In a school of 1800 pupils, how many would you expect to get flu this winter?

1. 130   2. $\frac{58}{320} = \frac{29}{160}$ 3. 800

Assessment questions

Try the following questions.

Starts: 8:54

Level 5 **1.** This fair spinner is spun. 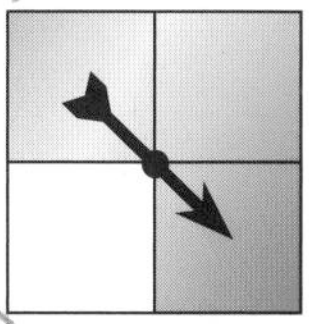
- **(a)** Is the spinner more likely to land on red or white? *Red*
  Give a reason for your answer. *Red has the majority of shaded squares*
- **(b)** Mark on the probability line below:
  - **(i)** the letter W to show the probability of the spinner landing on white
  - **(ii)** the letter B to show the probability of the spinner landing on black.

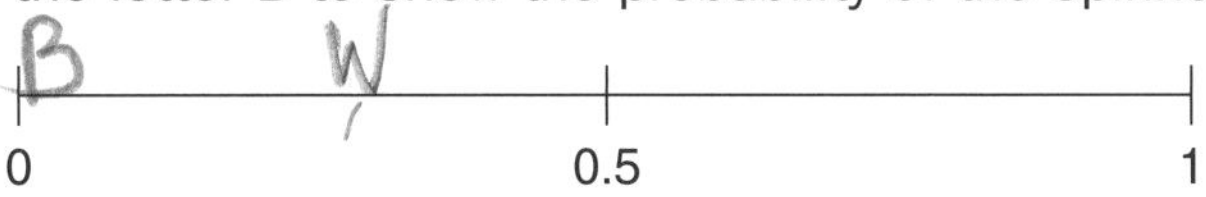

  B   W
  0   0.5   1

Level 5 **2.** This fair spinner is spun. Edward says that there is an equal chance of getting a 2 and a 3. Explain why he is wrong.
  2 has a bigger shaded area 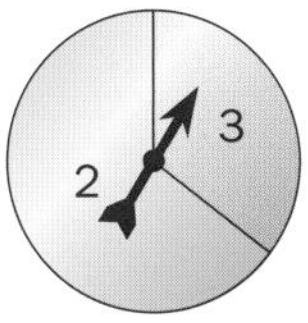

Level 5 **3.** Saima spins this spinner. 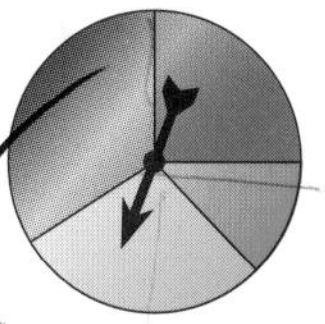
- **(a)** Which colour is she least likely to get and why?
  Red - least shaded area.
- **(b)** Saima thinks she has an equal chance to land on black and blue. Explain why she is wrong.
  Black has a larger shaded area
- **(c)** She also thinks that the probability of landing on red is $\frac{1}{4}$ because there are four colours. Explain why she is wrong.
  The colours arent equal   *Right or wrong. Answer then explain.*
- **(d)** Estimate, as a decimal, the probability of landing on blue. *0.25*

Level 6 **4.** A bag contains 7 red beads and 4 blue beads. A bead is taken at random. Find the probability that the bead is:
- **(a)** red *7/11*   **(b)** blue *4/11*   **(c)** yellow. *0/11*

Level 6 **5.** The diagram shows a spinner. 
- **(a)** What is the probability of obtaining a 3? *2/6*
- **(b)** What is the probability of obtaining an even number? *3/6*
- **(c)** What is the probability of obtaining a prime number? *4/6*
- **(d)** If the spinner is spun 120 times, estimate how many times it will land on a 6. *20*

Level 6 **6.** Richard and Tammy have three cards each.

Richard: 6 4 1   Tammy: 2 7 1

+	1	4	6
1	2	5	7
2	3	6	8
7	8	11	13

They each picked one of their own cards and added the scores of both cards.
- **(a)** Complete the sample-space diagram.
- **(b)** What is the probability of a total score of 6? *0/9*
- **(c)** What is the probability of an even score? *3/9*

149

Assessment questions

Level 6 **7.** Fiona can choose one piece of fruit and a drink from the list opposite. Write down all the possible outcomes.

a&c, o&c, b&c, a&l, o&l, b&l

Fruit	Drink
apple	coke
orange	lemonade
banana	

Level 6 **8.** The probability of passing an exam is 0.3
   (a) What is the probability of not passing the exam? 0.7
   (b) If 600 people take the exam, how many would you expect to pass? 180

Level 7 **9.** Matthew always has a packet of crisps with his lunch. The information below shows the probability that he has a particular flavour of crisps for lunch.

Salt and vinegar	0.2	Smoky bacon	0.25
Chicken	0.35	Cheese and onion	0.2

6.5/10

   (a) Calculate the probability of Matthew not having chicken flavour crisps. 6/54/10
   (b) Calculate the probability of Matthew having chicken or smoky bacon flavoured crisps.
   6/10

Level 7 **10.** When a dice was thrown 320 times, a 3 came up 62 times. What is the relative frequency of getting a 3?
   62/320   62/320

Level 8 **11.** The probability that Lucy is late for school is 0.3. The probability that Samuel is late for school is 0.4. What is the probability that:
   (a) they are both late? 0.3
   (b) only one of them is late? 0.1   Ⓒ

Level 8 **12.** On a stall at a summer fête, there are two bags of tickets. The first bag has 18 blue tickets and 12 red tickets. The second bag has 15 blue, 10 red and 20 yellow tickets.
   (a) Copy and complete the tree diagram.

18 15 | 33
12 10 | 22
       55

18 30   60
20 45
38 75   45
        45
        150

1st bag: Blue 18/30, Red 12/30
2nd bag: Blue 15/45, Red 10/45, Yellow 20/45; Blue 15/45, Red 10/45, Yellow 20/45

You pick one ticket from the first bag and one ticket from the second bag. If you pick two tickets of the same colour, you win a prize. If you pick a blue ticket and a yellow ticket, you get another go.

   (b) What is the probability of winning a prize? 55/150 → 11/30
   (c) What is the probability of getting another go? 38/75

150

Answers

Chapter 1

1. **(a)** 751 **(b)** 157

2. $\frac{4}{10}, \frac{10}{25}, \frac{8}{20}, \frac{20}{50}$

3. **(a)** 2, 5 **(b)** 1, 2, 12 **(c)** 1, 9, 16

4. 10°C

5. **(a)** ±12 **(b)** 8 **(c)** 4

6. £170 deposit
£780 in monthly instalments
Total: £950

7. 3.24, 3.241, 4.07, 4.105, 4.16

8. £3792

9. **(a)** 63.65 **(b)** 4.975 **(c)** $\frac{13}{21}$ **(d)** $1\frac{4}{11}$ or $\frac{15}{11}$

10.

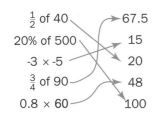

Column A	Column B
$\frac{1}{2}$ of 40	67.5
20% of 500	15
-3 × -5	20
$\frac{3}{4}$ of 90	48
0.8 × 60	100

11. £52

12. 100

13.

Fraction	$\frac{1}{5}$	$\frac{7}{20}$	$\frac{5}{8}$	$\frac{9}{20}$	$\frac{23}{100}$	$\frac{1}{3}$
Decimal	0.2	0.35	0.625	0.45	0.23	$0.\dot{3}$
Percentage	20%	35%	62.5%	45%	23%	$33.\dot{3}\%$

14. £8000, £12 000

15. 27%

16. The largest (700g) packet

17. 45.2%

18. £28.80

19. £6556.36

20. **(a)** $\frac{1}{4}$ **(b)** $2^7 = 128$ **(c)** 1 **(d)** ±4 **(e)** $\frac{1}{9}$

21. **(a)** 6×10^6 **(b) (i)** 6×10^{10} **(ii)** 6×10^{-6}

22. $x = 0.444\,444\,4...$ ①
$10x = 4.444\,444...$ ②
② - ① = $9x = 4$
$x = \frac{4}{9} = 0.\dot{4}$

23. £500

Chapter 2

1.

School	Number of pupils	Number of pupils to nearest	
		10	**100**
Appletown	1522	1520	1500
Beetown	1306	1310	1300
Nortown	2714	2710	2700
Duncetown	456	460	500

2. 45

3. **(a)** 44.25 **(b)** 34.79 **(c)** 22.36 **(d)** 4.5

4. £44.10

5. **(a)** 27 packets **(b)** 24 biscuits **(c)** £22.68

6. 7 boxes

7. Lucy is correct because the 3 × 7 is calculated before adding the 5.

8. **(a)** 10 **(b)** 2

9. **(a)** 300 × 40 = 12 000
(b) The order of magnitude is 10 times too small.
(c) 12 264

10. She counted the 82 as pounds not pence and did 4.24 + 82 instead of 4.24 + 0.82

11.
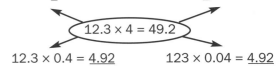

123 × <u>4</u> = 492   49.2 ÷ <u>4</u> = 12.3
12.3 × 4 = 49.2
12.3 × 0.4 = <u>4.92</u>   123 × 0.04 = <u>4.92</u>

12.

Number	2 d.p.	2 s.f.	1 s.f.
272.438	272.44	270	300
41.271	41.27	41	40
1.3728	1.37	1.4	1
147.525	147.53	150	100

13. **(a)** 0.451 33 **(b)** 214.3296 **(c)** 128.625
(d) 460.918 **(e)** 15.06

14. **(a)** 0.057 07 (5 d.p.)
(b) She did not use brackets when putting the second line in her calculator.

15. 1.145 because the reciprocal of the reciprocal of a number is the number itself.

16. **(a)** 24 500 000 **(b)** 25 499 999

17. **(a)** 339.5km **(b)** 340.5km

18. (a) $18.9 = 1.89 \times 10^1$ **(b)** 1.22×10^{-13}
(c) 2.23×10^{-8} **(d)** 6.73×10^{-8}

Chapter 3

1. £9.80

2.

Person	Number of books
Richard	n
Louise	$n + 5$
Rani	$3n + 15$
Total	$5n + 20$

3.

	$8p + 3$		
	$4p + 4$	$4p - 1$	
$2p + 3$	$2p + 1$	$2p - 2$	
p	$p + 3$	$p - 2$	p

4.

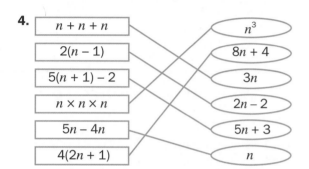

$n + n + n$ · n^3
$2(n - 1)$ · $8n + 4$
$5(n + 1) - 2$ · $3n$
$n \times n \times n$ · $2n - 2$
$5n - 4n$ · $5n + 3$
$4(2n + 1)$ · n

5.

p	$p + 2$	$2p - 1$	$3p$	$4(p - 2)$
2	4	3	6	0
5	7	9	15	12
10	12	19	30	32

6. 32

7. $15x - 20$

8. 12.6

9. (a) $n = 5$ **(b)** $y = 6$ **(c)** $p = 2$
(d) $y = -2$ **(e)** $y = 1$

10. (a) $5(2a + 3)$ **(b)** $3p^2(2p + 1)$

11. (a) $4n + 10$ **(b)** $4n + 10 = 22, n = 3$ **(c)** 7cm

12. $\frac{1}{a} + \frac{2}{b} = \frac{b + 2a}{ab}$ not $\frac{3}{a + b}$

13. (a) $a = 8, b = 12$ **(b)** $a = 25, b = 10$

14. $n = 5.4$

15. (a) $n < 4$ **(b)** $\frac{2}{5} \leqslant n < 2$

16. (a) $a^2 - a - 6$ **(b)** $16a^2 + 24a + 9$

17. $v = 10.9$ (1 d.p.)

18. (a) p^{11} **(b)** $4p^2$ **(c)** 1 **(d)** $p^{-2} = \frac{1}{p^2}$ **(e)** $16p^{12}$

19. (a) $(x + 6)(x + 3)$ **(b)** $(x - 2)(x - 3)$
(c) $(x + 9)(x - 9)$ **(d)** $(x + 6)(x - 4)$

Chapter 4

1. (a) 22, 25 **(b)** 32, 64 **(c)** 8, 4

2.

Input	2	4	5	7	9
Output	9	21	30	54	86

3. (a)

Pattern number (n)	1	2	3	4	5	6
Perimeter (cm)	6	10	14	18	22	26

(b) $4n + 2$ **(c)** 202cm

4. (a)

Rule	A	B	C	D	E	F
$x = 2$	✓	✗	✗	✓	✗	✗
$y = 2$	✗	✓	✓	✗	✗	✗
$y = x + 1$	✗	✓	✗	✗	✗	✓

(b) $x + y = 7$

5. (a) A, D, E **(b)** $y = x - 2$
(c) The line $y = 2x + 2$ goes through the points:
(-1, 0) (0, 2) (1, 4) (2, 6) (3, 8)
(d) Gradient = 2
(e) The lines intercept the y-axis according to the
constant in the equation.
e.g. $y = x + 3$ intercepts at (0, 3).

6. (a) $2n + 3$ **(b)** n^2 **(c)** $5n + 1$ **(d)** $\frac{1}{2n + 2}$

7. (a) 0820 **(b)** 16 minutes **(c)** 18km/h
(d) 15km/h

8. (a) $n^2 = n + n \times (n - 1)$
(b) $n^2 = 2 \times n + (n - 1) \times (n - 2) + (n - 2)$
(c) $n^2 = 2n + n^2 - 3n + 2 + n - 2$
$= n^2 + 3n - 3n + 2 - 2$
$= n^2$

9. (a) $y = 2x^2$ Ⓕ **(b)** $y = 3$ Ⓒ **(c)** $y = 2x^2$ Ⓕ
(d) $x + y = 10$ Ⓓ **(e)** $y = 3x - 2$ Ⓑ

10. A – graph 2 B – graph 3 C – graph 1 D – graph 4

11. A(0, 9), B(3, 0), C(-3, 0)

12. Graph 1 – label C ($y = x^3$);
Graph 2 – label A ($y = 2 - 5x$);
Graph 3 – label E ($y = \frac{2}{x}$);
Graph 4 – label F ($y = 16 - x^2$)

Chapter 5

1. (a) A, B, E, F **(b)** C or D, with explanation

2. (a) $r = 80°$ **(b)** $s = 65°$

3. 7.5km

4. (a)–(b)

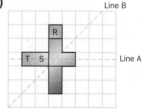

Line B
R
T S
Line A

5. (a)  **(b)** **(c)**

6. 128°

7. Forward 8; Turn right 120°; Forward 8; Turn right 120°; Forward 8; Stop

8. (a) $a = 140°$ $b = 105°$ $c = 115°$
   (b) $d = 55°$ $e = 125°$

9. (a) R from T = 070°   **(b)** R from P = 115°

10. 108°

11. $9^2 + 12^2 = 81 + 144 = 225 = 15^2$
Pythagoras' theorem only applies if the triangle is right-angled.

12. 84cm^2

13. (a) 10.0km (1 d.p.)   **(b)** 059° (nearest degree)

14. (a) 10cm   **(b)** 11.2cm (1 d.p.) **(c)** 10.3° (1 d.p.)

Chapter 6

1. Two isosceles triangles constructed – one with dimensions 5, 5, 7 and one with dimensions 7, 7, 5 (all in cm).

2. (a) Scale factor = 2
   (b) Centre of enlargement is at the bottom left-hand corner of the grid.

3. (a) 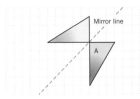   **(b)** 270°

4. (a)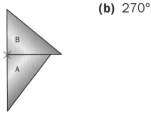

   (b) (i) Triangle should have moved 4 squares right and 2 squares down **(ii)** $\binom{4}{-2}$

5. 24 cubes

6. (a)–(b)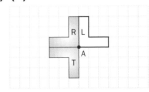

7. Each length of P should be three times the size of the original.

8.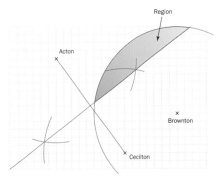

9.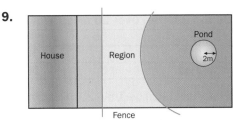

10. $p = 75$cm

11. (a) 8cm   **(b)** The triangles are similar because all three angles are the same.

Chapter 7

1. (a) Area = 7cm^2 **(b)** Perimeter = 16cm

2. (a) 23 hours 25 minutes   **(b)** 0315

3. $2\frac{1}{2}$ jugs of juice are needed.

4. (a) 5 centimetres   smallest
       5 metres
       5 kilometres
       5 miles   biggest
   (b) 2 milligrams   smallest
       2 grams
       2 pounds
       2 kilograms   biggest

5. 24km   **6. (a)** 20cm   **(b)** 22cm   **7.** £755.79

8. 3.4%   **9.** £26.25

10. Because 1m^2 = 10 000cm^2 **11.** 2.5cm (1 d.p.)

12. (a) Volume = 201cm^3 (3 s.f.)
   (b) Area = 100.5cm^2 (1 d.p.)
   (c) The scale factor is 3. The volume scale factor is cubed, i.e. $3^3 = 27$. The volume of the enlarged tin is 27 times bigger.

13. Area of cross-section = $4x^2$
Volume = $4x^2 \times 5x = 20x^3$

Chapter 8

1.

Type of TV programme	Tally	Frequency

2.

Type of TV programme	Tally	Frequency
Comedy	LH1 IIII	9
Soap	LH1 II	7
Film	LH1	5
		21

3. (a)

Score	Tally	Frequency
1–10	|||	3
11–20	ᕼᕼ ||	7
21–30	ᕼᕼ	5
31–40	ᕼᕼ		6
41–50	ᕼᕼ ||||	9

(b) 41–50

4. (a) The groups overlap, for example which box would a 30-year-old person tick?
(b) 'Sometimes', 'occasionally' and 'often' can mean different things to different people.

5.

	Up to 20 miles	Over 20 miles	Total
Car	45	55	100
Train	120	30	150
Total	165	85	250

30 people had travelled more than 20 miles by train.

6. (a) Biased – the people who live near the supermarket are more likely to go.
(b) Not biased – each person has an equally likely chance of being chosen.
(c) Biased – not everybody uses trains, so each person in the population does not have an equal chance of being chosen.
(d) Biased – most 10–18 year olds do not go shopping for food.

Chapter 9

1. (a) 6 hours **(b)** Wednesday **(c)** 11 hours
(d) Emma watched 3 + 8 = 11 hours and William watched 4 + 5 = 9 hours, so Emma watched more television.

2. (a) 12.5°C **(b)** Thursday **(c)** Tuesday and Friday

3. (a) Mean = 13.2 (1 d.p.) **(b)** Median = 10.5
(c) Range = 33

4. 12 and 4

5. (a) 5000 **(b)** 2500 **(c)** 1000
(d) In Town B, there are 900 over 59 year olds compared with 2500 over 59 year olds in Town A. Hence Archie is wrong.
(e) In Town A there are 3750 0–19 year olds compared with 200 0–19 year olds in Town B. Hence the new school should be built in Town A.

6. (a) As the temperature increases, more ice lollies are sold. (Positive correlation)
(b) As the temperature increases, fewer cups of tea are sold. (Negative correlation)

7. (a)

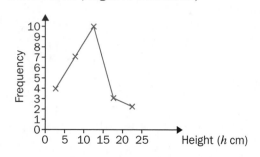

(b) Modal class $10 \leqslant h < 15$
(c) Mean = 11.0cm (1 d.p.)

8. (a)

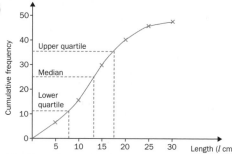

(b) Median about 12.8cm
(c) Interquartile range about 9cm
(d)

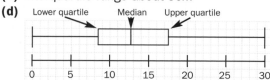

Chapter 10

1. (a) Red because there are three squares compared with one white.
(b) (i)–(ii)

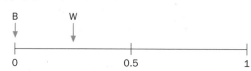

2. He is wrong because the 2 has a larger area so the spinner is more likely to land on it.

3. (a) Red because it is the smallest section.
(b) Black is a larger section so there is more chance of landing on it.
(c) She is wrong because all four colours are not equally likely.
(d) 0.25

4. (a) $\frac{7}{11}$ **(b)** $\frac{4}{11}$ **(c)** 0

5. (a) $\frac{2}{6} = \frac{1}{3}$ **(b)** $\frac{3}{6} = \frac{1}{2}$ **(c)** $\frac{4}{6} = \frac{2}{3}$ **(d)** 20

6. (a)

+	1	4	6
1	2	5	7
2	3	6	8
7	8	11	13

(b) $\frac{1}{9}$ **(c)** $\frac{4}{9}$

7. apple, coke   orange, coke
banana, coke   apple, lemonade
orange, lemonade banana, lemonade

8. (a) 0.7 **(b)** 180   **9. (a)** 0.65 **(b)** 0.6

10. $\frac{62}{320} = \frac{31}{160}$ **11. (a)** 0.12 **(b)** 0.46

12. (a)

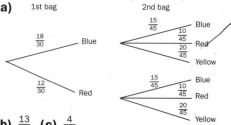

(b) $\frac{13}{45}$ **(c)** $\frac{4}{15}$

Glossary

Angle a measurement of turn

Approximation a rough answer; approximations are made by rounding off numbers

Area the amount of space a 2-D shape covers

Average speed the total distance travelled divided by the total time taken

Bar graph a diagram made up of a set of bars, of equal width. The lengths are proportional to a set of frequencies

Bearing an angle measured from the North in a clockwise direction; bearings have three figures

Bias an event that is more likely to give one outcome than another

Bisect cut exactly in half

Brackets symbols which show those terms that should be treated together

Capacity a measure of the amount of space inside a 3-D object

Circumference the distance around the outside edge of a circle

Class interval a grouping of statistical data

Coefficient this is the number in front of a letter in an algebraic expression

Congruent shapes figures that are the same size and the same shape

Continuous data data that is obtained by measuring

Cumulative frequency this is found by doing a running total of the frequencies

Data collective name for pieces of information, often obtained from an experiment or survey

Degree a unit for measuring angles

Denominator the number on the bottom of a fraction

Density the mass per unit volume of a solid

Diagonal a line joining any two vertices of a shape

Diameter a straight line that passes through the centre of a circle

Discrete data data that can be counted

Edge where two faces meet in a 3-D shape

Elevation the view of a 3-D shape from its front or side

Equation a statement that two or more things are equal

Evaluate work out the value of an expression

Exterior angles the angles on the outside of a polygon

Face one of the flat surfaces of a 3-D shape

Factor a number that divides exactly into another number

Factorise separate an expression into its factors

Formula a mathematical expression that is used to solve problems

Frequency the number of times that an event has occurred

Frequency polygons joins the midpoints of class intervals for grouped or continuous data

Gradient the slope of a line in relation to the positive direction of the x-axis

Horizontal a line that goes straight across; it is parallel to the Earth's surface

Hypotenuse the longest side of a right-angled triangle

Hypothesis a statement that can be tested to see if it is true

Independent events if two events have no effect on each other, they are said to be independent

Index the power to which a quantity is raised

Inequality a statement that two or more things are not equal

Integer a positive or negative whole number

Intercept the point at which a graph cuts the y-axis

Interior angles the angles on the inside of a polygon

Isosceles triangle a triangle with two equal sides and two equal angles

Linear consisting of a line or having one dimension; a linear graph is a straight-line graph; a linear expression is one such as $2x + 3$, which on a graph gives a straight line

Line graph a graph formed by joining points with straight lines

Locus the locus of a point is the set of all possible positions that the point can occupy, subject to some given conditions or rule

Lowest terms a fraction is in its lowest terms when it cannot be cancelled down any further

Glossary

Mapping a relationship between one group of numbers and another group of numbers

Mean the sum of all the values divided by the number of values used

Median the middle value when a set of numbers is put in order of size

Mode the value that occurs most often

Multiples the numbers in the multiplication tables, e.g. multiples of 5 are 5, 10, 15, 20, etc. since 5 will divide exactly into these numbers

Multiplier scale factor

Mutually exclusive events that cannot happen at the same time

Net a flat shape that can be folded into a 3-D solid

Numerator the top part of a fraction

Outcomes the possible results of a statistical experiment or other activity involving uncertainty

Parallel lines lines that never meet; they are always the same distance apart

Percentage a fraction with a denominator of 100

Perimeter distance around the outside edge of a shape

Perpendicular two lines are perpendicular to each other if they meet at 90°

Plan the view of a 3-D shape when looked down on from above

Polygon a plane figure that has three or more straight sides; a regular polygon has all sides and all angles equal

Prime number a number that only has two factors: 1 and itself

Product the result of two or more numbers multiplied together

Quadrilateral a polygon with four sides

Questionnaire a sheet with questions, used to collect data

Radius distance from the centre of a circle to the circumference

Range the difference between the highest and lowest numbers in a set of data

Ratio a comparison between two quantities, which are measured in the same units

Reciprocal the reciprocal of a number $\frac{a}{x}$ is $\frac{x}{a}$

Relative frequency this is used as an estimate of a probability

Scale factor the multiplier when a shape is enlarged or reduced in size

Sequence a set of numbers with a pattern

Similar two or more figures are similar when they are the same shape but not the same size; one is the enlargement of the other

Standard index form a way of writing very large or very small numbers; they are written in the form $a \times 10^n$ where $1 < a < 10$ and n is an integer

Substitution replacing a letter with its numerical value

Term one of the parts of an expression

Triangle a polygon with three straight sides

Variable a quantity that can take a range of values

Vector a quantity that has both size and direction

Vertical a line is vertical if it goes straight up and down and is at 90° to the horizontal.

x-**axis** the horizontal axis

y-**axis** the vertical (up) axis

Notes

Notes

Index